# STEPS IN TECHNOLOGY

**R. Bateman and T. Hewitt**

London Melbourne Sydney Auckland Johannesburg

Hutchinson Education

An imprint of Century Hutchinson Ltd
62–65 Chandos Place, London WC2N 4NW

Century Hutchinson Australia Pty Ltd
PO Box 496, 16–22 Church Street, Hawthorn,
Victoria 3122, Australia

Century Hutchinson New Zealand Ltd
PO Box 40–086, Glenfield, Auckland 10, New Zealand

Century Hutchinson South Africa (Pty) Ltd
PO Box 337, Bergvlei, 2012 South Africa

First published 1989

© T. Hewitt and R. Bateman 1988
Text set in Plantin and Future
by Hope Services, Abingdon
Reproduced, printed and bound in Great Britain by
Hazell Watson & Viney Limited
Member of BPCC plc
Aylesbury, Bucks, England
Designed by Raynor Design

**British Library Cataloguing in Publication Data**
Hewitt, T.
   Steps in technology.
   1. Technology
   I. Title   II. Bateman, R.
   600   T47
   ISBN 0–09–172984–X

# Acknowledgements

To our families, Ben, Jess, Lucy and Sue Hewitt, Tony, Sue,
Liz and Sheila Bateman, thank you all for the tea, biscuits,
encouragement and unfailing patience. Also to Thomas
Charles Jones for his invaluable creative contribution to
artwork and design at manuscript stage and to Cally James
for photographic assistance. Finally to our publishers, Pat
Rowlinson and editor Ruth Holmes.

   Acknowledgement is due to the following for permission
to reproduce photographs: Alton Towers Leisure Park 1.3E;
Barnaby's Picture Library 5.1A, 5.1B, 7.4E, 9.1A, 10.1Aii, iv,
10.2B, 10.3A, 10.4B, 10.4C, Great technological achievements,
Safety C; Robin Birkett 5.1B, 7.4D, 8.2B, 8.3A, 9.1A, 10.4C;
Ceco International 8.2Ci; Cooper Tools Ltd 8.2Civ; Sally and
Richard Greenhill 6.4D, Safety A, B; Terry Hewitt Safety E;
Murex Welding Products Ltd 8.2Cii, iii; Ontario Science
Center 9.1A; Oxford Scientific Films 10.4C; RHM 10.4D; Ann
Ronan Picture Library 6.3B, 7.1D, 10.1Ai, iii; RS
Components 9.3B; H. Samuel 10.4C, 10.4D; Science Photo
Library/Tim Davis 9.3D; Science Photo Library/Malcolm
Felding 9.3D; Science Photo Library/Adam Hart 9.3D;
Science Photo Library/Dick Luria 9.3D; Science Photo
Library/Paul Shambroom 9.3D; Science Photo Library/US
Department of Energy 5.1B; Vauxhall Motors Ltd 7.1F.

# Contents

# 1.1   What is technology?

The word technology is made up of two parts:

**1** *Techno* – which is similar to the word technical. They both come originally from the Greek word *tekhne* meaning art. Also, *tekton* means builder or carpenter in Greek, so it has something to do with practical arts which we now call 'skills'. (Cartoon **A**)

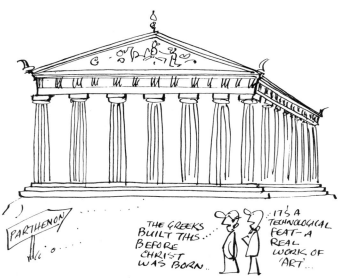

**A**   *Technological art*

**2** *-logy* – again from Greek (busy people in languages!). *Logia* means 'to speak of' and *logy* has come to mean 'study of'. So:

> Earth study = Geo logy.
> Life study = Bio logy.
> Skills study = Techno logy. (Cartoon **B**)

**B**   *People and what they study*

So technology is the study of skills (practical arts) and has grown to include the study of practical materials, skills and knowledge. But technology is more than just a study of theory, it is practical. It is the **application of technical and scientific knowledge and skills**. A person who 'does' technology is called a **technologist**.

Technologists study advances made in science and engineering and then use this knowledge to solve everyday problems in many things. They examine the problem, read about what may help solve it, dream up several possible solutions, choose the best, make it, and then test it to see if it can be improved. Cartoon **C** shows the process of technology.

**C**   *The process of technology*

Technology solves real problems. Technology starts with scientific research, includes market research and ends with a satisfied customer. For example, an elderly person asks the technologist for a remote control for his TV. The technologist checks with scientists what methods could be used, asks market researchers how many he can sell and what he should charge, then makes it, sells it and retires on the fortune he has made! The products of technology must work, be affordable and look good.

There are various different branches of technology. The technology of food may look at how to put new flavours into crisps, or how to give crisps a good flavour without artificial chemicals. The technology of machines may look at how to put a new heart pacemaker into place. The technology of building may look at how to build Stonehenge and so on. Cartoon **D** shows some technologists with their typical products.

*Test tube baby*

*BIOTECHNOLOGIST*

*BACON CRISPS*

*FOOD TECHNOLOGIST*

*The biggest crane in the world*

*Ice*

*ARTIFICIAL SALT*

*CHEMICAL TECHNOLOGIST*

*Heart Pacemaker*

*ENGINEERING TECHNOLOGIST*

*MEDICAL TECHNOLOGIST*

**D**  *Technologists and products*

## ▶ Things to do

▶ **1**  **a**  Copy the definition of technology given in the text.
    **b**  Get a dictionary and copy its definition of technology.

▶ **2**  Rearrange the phrases in the following sentences so that the sentences make sense and describe the process of technology.
    **a**  with a problem . . . technology starts.
    **b**  solutions are . . . information is found . . . before . . . proposed.
    **c**  best . . . the . . is made . . . solution.
    **d**  improved . . . the final solution . . . after testing . . . is often.
    **e**  should be . . . at the end of . . . your problem . . . the process . . . solved.

▶ **3**  **Learn a skill – How to see a problem as an opportunity to make something people might want**

    As you read this book you should try to notice problems around you (lessons are too long, desks are too small, seat is wrong shape and so on).

    Here are some guidelines to thinking up a problem using technology.
    **a**  Am I comfortable? Too hot, too cold, sitting down awkwardly, cramped.
    **b**  Do I need anything to make work better or easier? Writing, cutting, colouring, talking.
    **c**  Am I sensing things properly? Seeing, hearing, feeling, talking, touching.
    **d**  Entertainment.
    **e**  Eating/drinking.

    How could it be . . . easier, more fun, smoother, quieter, safer, more interesting, more stylish, nicer to look at, more tidy, tastier?

▶ **4**  **Think of a problem** (NO, an opportunity!) Think up a problem for the medical technologist (a new style walking frame, a baby alarm, a bed-making machine). Design four solutions to this problem.
    **a**  So it works. (Technical)
    **b**  So that people will want to buy it. (Market awareness)

▶ **5**  **Solve a problem**   Design a TV remote control unit. You must not use electricity. It must be made of bits and pieces of scrap material, milk bottle tops, the inside of toilet rolls, sellotape and string. Draw five or six rough ideas and one neat, detailed, 'best' solution.

# 1.2 Technology and technologists

farming – old person cuts grain with scythe

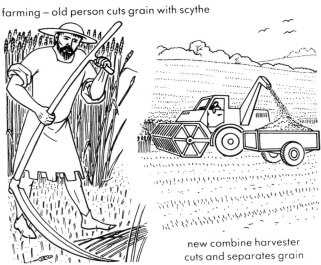

new combine harvester
cuts and separates grain

**A** *Technology helps people*

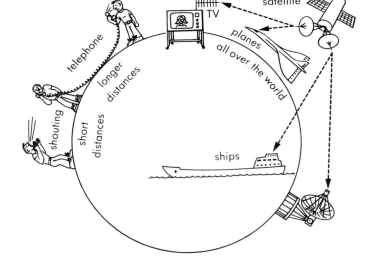

Technology helps people by:

1 Making work easier for them (diagram **A**).
2 Extending their senses (sight, sound, smell, etc).
3 Improving communications (diagram **A**).

Technological advances have changed the world in many ways, and diagram **B** shows some of these changes. Most people see these things (or most of them!) as good. Cartoon **C** shows the development of one technology which some people see as not so good.

Technology is not good or bad, it is neutral. But it can be used for positive (good) or negative (bad) motives. Technologists design and make things. It is politicians who decide whether things like satellites are used for peace keeping or war making, communication or spying. A technologist does not make these decisions.

A technologist should have:

1 Imagination – to think up new solutions to problems and to visualize how pieces will fit together, how parts will move and what effect forces will have.
2 Logic – to think about problems one step at a time, to appreciate what is important and what is irrelevant, to plan work and use common sense.
3 Concentration – not to be distracted from the task in hand.
4 A good memory – to remember and learn from personal experience and the experience of others.

**B** *Technological advances*

5 A sense of responsibility – to work as a member of a team.
6 Perseverance – to cope with 'boring' parts of a job and to see a problem through to completion.

A technologist should know about mathematics, science, craft, and design. Technology is how these studies and skills are all brought together to make things.

## ▶ *Things to do*

▶ **1 a** Study diagram **A**:
*Either* draw the part of it which you like best, *or* invent another part of this cartoon using your own ideas.
  **b** Write two sentences about it to explain how technology helps people.

▶ **2** List six personal qualities (e.g. imagination, memory) of a good technologist. Give one example when you have needed each one to start and finish making something useful.

▶ **3 Learn a skill – How to get information from a cartoon strip**

It is interesting to look at technological changes from the past through to the present and future. Cartoon **C** and diagram **D** do this.
  **a** Write five sentences to explain the development of buttons through the ages.
  **b** Draw the fifth diagram to show how a button might work in *the future*.

▶ **4 Think of a problem** Do you ever have a problem fastening up your clothes with buttons, zips or Velcro? If you do, describe by words, cartoons or diagrams what it is. If not, think up another problem you may sometimes have with clothes and describe it clearly.

▶ **5 Solve a problem** *Either* solve the problem you described in Task **4**, *or* design a device which will make life easier for you (e.g. a machine to copy 100 lines). This device must be made from household scrap (yoghurt pots, toilet rolls, straws, bottle tops etc). Aim for it to be useful, reliable and cheap.

*C   Advances?*

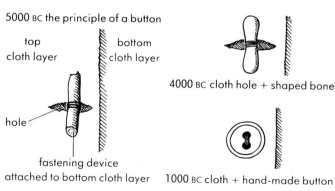

5000 BC the principle of a button

top cloth layer                 bottom cloth layer

hole

fastening device attached to bottom cloth layer

4000 BC cloth hole + shaped bone

1000 BC cloth + hand-made button

1900 AD cloth hole with stamped plastic button

**?**
2100 AD the future?

*D   The button – past, present and future*

# 1.3 Technology for fun

Technology is not deadly serious and boring. Technology can be fun (see cartoon **A**). Toys have always been made using the latest technology, from the Ancient Greek steam machines (cartoon **B**) to today's computers (cartoon **C**).

The best technologists need a keen sense of humour. One of the pioneers of steam was so delighted when he drove his steam powered vehicle for the first time that he drove it straight to the nearest inn. He left the fire burning while he and his friends celebrated and was gone so long that it boiled dry and the whole thing exploded! His celebration was short lived!

Richard Trevithick's and George Stevenson's steam engines were used to provide 'fairground' style rides for paying customers. They demonstrated the serious side of their 'new' technology by letting people have fun (see cartoon **D**). Modern fairgrounds and theme parks use quite complex technology to provide fun and thrills (see photograph **E**).

**A**  Technology can be fun

**B**  Technological toy of the past

**C**  Modern technological toy

**D** Early fairground rides

## ▶ *Things to do*

▶ **1** Decide which diagram you like best from cartoons **A, B, C**. Draw it and add some more detail to it.

▶ **2** Study the cartoons. Write a short (half page) 'History of technology for fun'.

▶ **3** **Learn a skill – How to use natural materials for fun**
Diagram **F** shows how to make a peashooter using the hawthorn buds and cowparsley stems found in most hedgerows. Draw a diagram or cartoon strip to show how it works.

▶ **4** **Think of a problem** Describe a 'Technology for fun' idea that you would like to develop.

▶ **5** **Solve a problem** *Either* show how you could design and make something to solve the problem found in Task **4**. *Or* plan a 'Technological fairground of the future'. Draw an overall view and the details of one particular 'ride'.

**E** Technological monsters for fun

**F** Make a pea-shooter

# 1.4    Problems to be solved

Technology has not solved all the problems of the
world. Diagrams **A–F** show a few waiting for
someone like you to come up with solutions for
them. Find a good one and you could become
very successful.

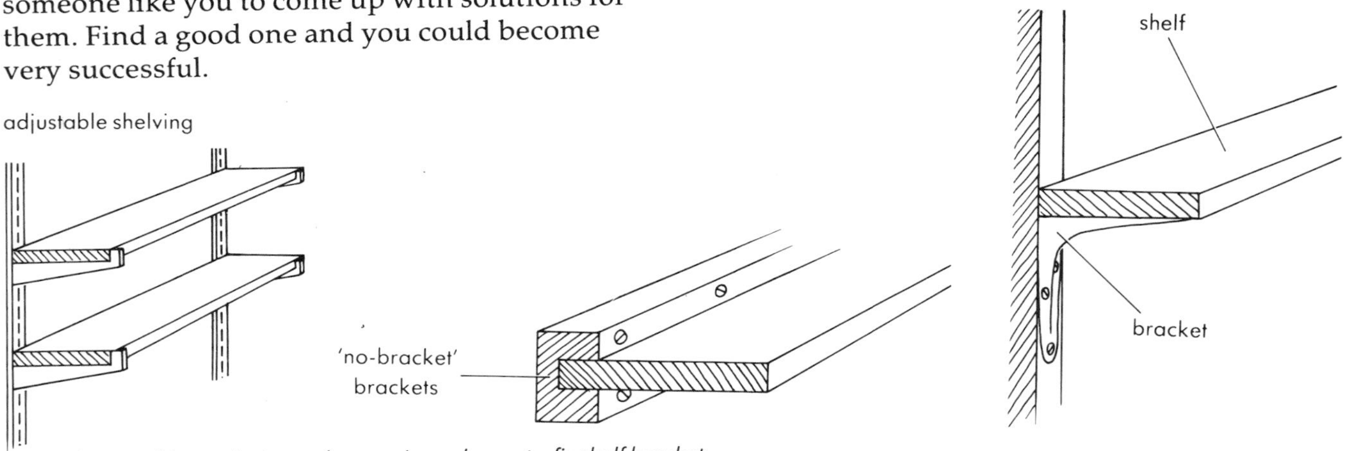

adjustable shelving

shelf

bracket

'no-bracket'
brackets

**A**   *Indoor problem – design a cheap universal easy-to-fix shelf bracket*

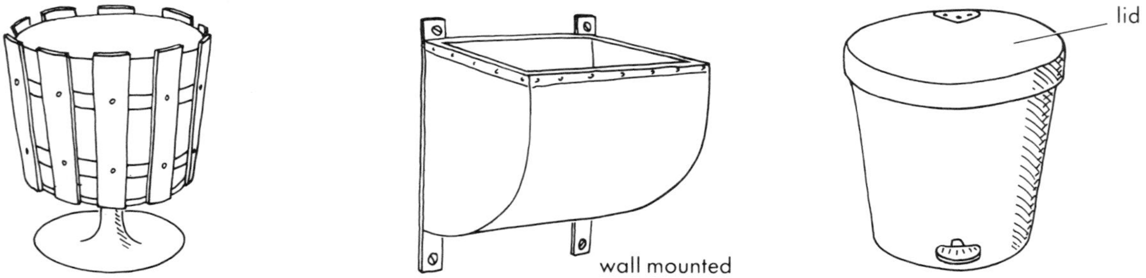

lid

wall mounted

**B**   *Outdoor problem – design a vandal-proof litter bin for schools*

C5

**C**   *Moving problem – design a cheap form of transport for 12–15-year-olds*

**D**  Insoluble problem? Designing an indestructible toy for children under 5 years of age

**E**  Big problem – design a combined TV, radio, audio, compact disc, video, computer and tea-making alarm clock

**F**  Small problem – design an eraser which does not leave any bits behind on the page

## ▶ Things to do

▶ **1**  Choose one of the problems on these pages. Make a clear drawing of the problem and try to describe the problem in a short paragraph.

▶ **2**  A common problem for technologists is spelling! Copy out this list of words, but this time with the proper spellings.
Erazer   vidoe   brackett   concreet   ajustable.

▶ **3**  **Learn a skill – Lateral thinking**   How thick is a page in this book? Can't measure it with a ruler? Then measure the thickness of 40 pages (e.g. 80 sides, from side 10 to side 90) with your ruler. Then simply divide by 40.
e.g. 40 pages = 4 millimetres, so
1 page = $^4/_{40}$ = $^1/_{10}$ millimetre

▶ **4**  **Think of a problem**   Find a problem, not on this page, which you feel could earn you a fortune if you could solve it. It should be for use in schools by teachers *or* pupils.

▶ **5**  **Solve a problem**   Choose any *one* of the problems on this page. Talk it over with your friends. Then try to work out a solution and make a neat drawing of it.

# 2.1  How is a problem solved?

Technology is about finding solutions to problems. Some problems are easier to solve than others (see cartoon **A**). One problem that a technologist could be asked to solve is to design a device for transporting young children. Diagram **B** shows some existing solutions to this problem.

Before you can solve a problem you have to be sure *exactly* what the problem is. In technological terms defining the problem is done by writing a **design brief**. The design brief for this problem could be:
'Design a device to transport young children'.

You need more information before you start designing your solution to this problem. How many children? How old? and so on. These questions are answered in the **specification**:

1   Carry one child.
2   Maximum load 20 kg.
3   Comfortable.
4   Weather resistant.
5   Easy to use.
6   Must not tip.
7   . . . Add as many as you wish.

**Information** on existing solutions (remember diagram **B**?) is useful at this stage. Then you should try to think of several **possible solutions**. This should include possible layouts (diagram **C**), wheels if necessary (diagram **D**), ergonomics (comfortableness! cartoon **E**), types of materials e.g. wood, plastic, metal, and any other considerations that you think are important.

From all of these possibilities the **best** is **selected**. Work is planned, perhaps a model made and finally the design is **realised** or made. After this comes the stage of **evaluation**, does it work? etc. This may lead to changes or **modifications**, which will also need to be planned, realised and modified. Solving one problem may lead to others!

Diagram **F** shows the main stages in problem solving.

This has been a simple example. We have not considered additions like awnings, racks for shopping, folding sections, TV and stereo to keep the baby amused etc, etc! But you should have some idea of how to design the ultimate baby transport vehicle.

**A**   *Solving problems*

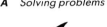

**B**   *How to transport young children*

**C**   *Possible layouts*

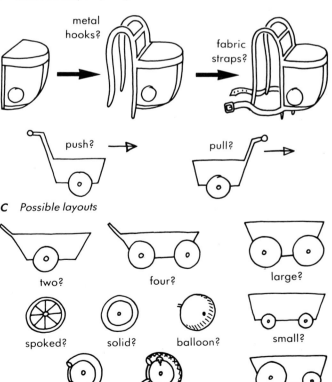

**D**   *Wheels*

*E  Ergonomics*

*F  Problem solving*

## ▶ Things to do

▶ **1**  Put a title 'Problem solving', then copy flow diagram **F**.

▶ **2**  Talk with your friends to match these 'heads' and 'tails'. Then write them out neatly.

| HEADS | TAILS |
|---|---|
| **a**  A design brief is | designs lead to the choice of the best. |
| **b**  Details of the problem | a statement of the problem. |
| **c**  Several alternative | and testing may lead to modifications. |
| **d**  Another word for | are described in the specification. |
| **e**  Evaluation | making is realisation. |

▶ **3**  **Learn a skill – How to propose alternatives**
For example, consider the task of 'Design *three* different alternative layouts for a child transporter'.

Think of some different ways of shifting things. Think of how animals move or push or pull things. Think of machines which shift things, or throw things, or take things into space.

Let your imagination run wild. It doesn't matter if your ideas are crazy nine times out of ten. Your tenth might just be a winner! Go for it!

When you think you have a good idea, try to 'sell' it to a friend. If they think it might be O.K. draw it. You have three to draw, so don't spend too long about it. Maybe your brain will keep working and you will get the real winner when you are 30 years old!

▶ **4**  **Think of a problem**   Find a problem connected with young children and write a design brief and specification for it. (Feeding? Sitting at table? Sleeping? Nappy changing? Crying?)

▶ **5**  **Solve a problem**   Rex and Honey are two dogs who would like you to design a super de luxe kennel for them. There must be all the normal features, such as under floor heating, smellovision set, and bone dispenser. Now add some original ideas and room for guests (Muppet, Bubbles, Jamie, Mitzi and Fritzi are frequent visitors. Their owners, Dick and Terry, are often in the doghouse!). Produce several designs and select the best.

# 2.2 Problem solving in industry

**A** Market research

In industry, problems are identified by market research staff. They find out from potential customers what they want (and how much they are prepared to pay!). Techniques used in market research include those shown in cartoon **A**.

Directors of companies use this information to help them decide on a **design brief** which is a brief outline of the problem (see cartoon **B**). The development and research team take this brief a stage further by writing the detailed **specification** (see cartoon **C**). This specification will include costs. Some people want cheap products which they know will not last. Some people want the best and are prepared to pay for it. See cartoon **D**.

The next stage is **investigation**. What size, what shape, what parts of existing products can be used (or modified)? What new parts will be needed? Can we make all the parts or should we 'buy in' from an outside contractor? Can we make it for the target price? Can we sell it? (There was very little wrong with a small electric vehicle called the Sinclair C5, it just would not sell. The research team had done its work but the investigation of what people would buy was too optimistic.)

The design team uses the results of the investigation to produce **alternative designs**. These are likely to include drawings, models and mock-ups. These will be used to help the directors select the **best** design (see cartoon **E**). The best may be the cheapest, or the easiest to produce, or the best looking, or the fastest, or the strongest. The decision about what is 'best' is very difficult to make!

**B** A design brief

Once the decision has been made detailed drawings are made in the drawing office. There will be **working drawings**, **parts lists** and **cutting lists**. Then production staff will plan how to make the various components.

When the components have been made, they have to be assembled to make the first model – the **prototype**. This is the **realisation** of the **design** (see cartoon **F**).

This is followed by **evaluation**. Does it work? Does it break? How well does it answer all the points in the specification? If tests show faults these have to be put right. The design must be **modified** before the final finished product is sent to sales staff who sell it to the customer.

If it sells everyone is happy – customer and company. If not, all of this time, money and energy are wasted. No sales means no work!

**C** A design specification

**D** Getting what you pay for

**F** Design realisation

## ▶ *Things to do*

▶ **1** Study cartoons **B** and **E**. They show a firm's directors at times before and during an industrial project. Draw either of the cartoons, or your own version of one of them. Make sure you label all your directors, and give the firm a name.

▶ **2** Study the specification for the portable pop video player in cartoon **C**. Draw your own version of it, putting the items in the order which you think customers would most look for. Add in three other specifications to make the list up to ten.

▶ **3** **Learn a skill – How to judge 'quality'**
Look around the room at pencils, pens, pencil cases, bags, desks, walls and blackboards. In a group of three, talk over the quality of each. (For example, pencil – flow quality, lead breaks easily, wood dents, paint flakes, rubber wears down before pencil is used up.) Record your views. Decide whether this equipment is what is needed. Make recommendations if you think not. Don't forget 'value for money'.

▶ **4** **Think of a problem**   Think up another new product, like the portable video player. Decide who would buy it. Work out a simple set of questions for the market research. Try it out on some classmates you do not know very well.

▶ **5** **Solve a problem**   Advertising a new product is crucial. One way of reaching potential customers for a portable pop video machine is through commercial radio. Write a script for a 30 second radio advertisement.

# 2.3   Developing ideas

Many people dream of being inventors and making money from their original inventions. The problem is that you can't just tell your mind to create an original idea. What you can do is to encourage your mind by *thinking* about a problem, *reading* about it and *studying* every aspect of it. This is where writing a specification can be helpful. A specification breaks the main problem into smaller parts: aspects of the brief. (See cartoon **A**.)

**Inventive** thinking is about studying a problem to gain a 'feel' for it. If you fill your mind with the 'feel' for the problem and then relax and think of other things your subconscious mind will often go on thinking about the problem. Sometimes the solution to a problem will come in a flash of inspiration from your subconscious.

Fifteen artists, mathematicians and musicians were asked what they were doing when they had their 'flash' of creative inspiration. Table **B** shows the results. A mixture of concentration followed by relaxation helps inventive, creative thinking. Sitting at a desk helps you fill your mind with the parts of the problem that your subconscious needs to work on later. One important thing to remember is that your mind works in pictures not words. This is why drawing (particularly in three dimensions) is so important to the technologist (see cartoon **C**).

**Artistic** thinking is about making things 'look' right. This is difficult to define because people's tastes are different. The style of designs changes over the years and so does what looks right in, for example, clothes (see cartoon **D**). Technologists always try to make their products attractive and **aesthetically** pleasing. Often existing designs can be improved by a slight redesigning of style.

**Common sense** thinking may tell you that the wonderful design of your imagination, perfectly made and artistically pleasing, will cost too much. In that case, is it worth making? Is it worthwhile creating a new style typewriter when everyone has a computer? Would anyone buy a beautifully designed, reliable black and white television if it cost ten times the price of a colour television? One company decided to mechanise assembly of its product but forgot that loading the machines needed people power. It finished up with the same number of workers, a very

**A**   *Breaking down the problem*

| | |
|---|---|
| Half-asleep in bed | 4 |
| Out walking | 3 |
| Travelling | 3 |
| In church | 2 |
| Eating | 1 |
| Sitting by the fire | 2 |

**B**   *Inspiring places*

expensive assembly line and lost money because no one had used their common sense.

In industry technologists tend to work in one of three departments:

1   Projects – inventive, creative thinkers trying out new ideas (e.g. with Fischer–Technic or Meccano).
2   Development – artistic thinkers testing and improving original ideas.
3   Production – common sense, logical thinkers streamlining production techniques to make the final product.

Which type of technological thinking are you best at?

C   *Thinking in pictures*

## ▶ Things to do

▶ **1**   Put a heading 'Ideas in Industry'. Read the whole of the opposite page. Then say which type of thinker you reckon you are, out of the three types shown.

▶ **2**   Explain the differences between:
   **a**  inventive thinking,
   **b**  artistic thinking,
   **c**  common sense thinking.

▶ **3**   **Learn a skill – How to 'brainstorm'**
One way of getting a good idea is to throw lots of ideas at a group. Work with a group of between three and five on the problem shown in diagram **E** and Task **5**. First, quickly (and without thinking of common sense answers), brainstorm 20 possible solutions. Just write down the first two letters of each idea. Later you can write any sensible ideas down for your records.

▶ **4**   **Think of a problem**   Be an inventor. Design a new style board game. It *must* be original.

▶ **5**   **Solve a problem**   Produce either an inventive, artistic or common sense solution to the problem of opening a garage door (see diagram **E**).
Examples:
Inventive – drive over high explosive, flash focussed through magnifying glass to burn string holding door closed.
Artistic – an ergonomic door handle/lock.
Logical – **1** Leave car.  **2** Get key. **3** Unlock.
**4** Open door...

ELIZABETHAN DRESS

VICTORIAN DRESS

1940's DRESS

1960's DRESS

**D**   *Changing design styles*

**E**   *Brainstorming*

# 2.4 Planning and testing

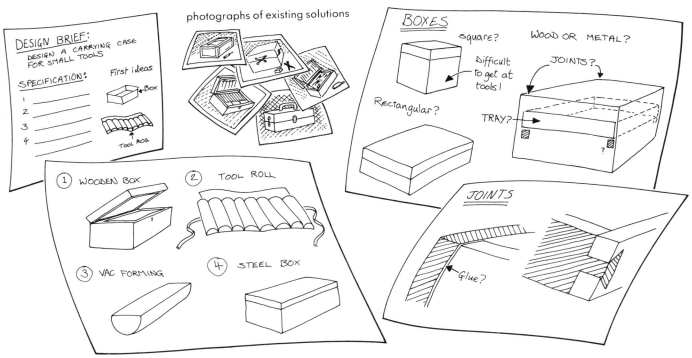

**A** *Design sheets*

Design sheets will include many ideas, notes, drawings, sketches and so on. From this mass of information (see diagram **A**) *one* 'best' design has to be chosen. One useful aid to selecting the best is to mark various aspects of the solution (cost, ease of manufacture, reliability etc). Table **B** shows a choice table of this type. Whether design 1 or 4 is chosen will depend on how important each aspect is.

| Design | Cost | Ease of manufacture | Reliability | Appearance | Efficiency | Ease of use | Total |
|--------|------|---------------------|-------------|------------|------------|-------------|-------|
| 1 | 5 | 5 | 3 | 5 | 5 | 1 | 24 |
| 2 | 1 | 1 | 1 | 2 | 1 | 1 | 7 |
| 3 | 3 | 2 | 3 | 3 | 2 | 3 | 16 |
| 4 | 1 | 5 | 5 | 5 | 5 | 5 | 26 |

**Marks**  0 = Poor  5 = Very good

**B**  *Choice table*

At this stage it may be helpful to make a model out of **paper, card** or **clay** to help you **visualise** what the final product will look like. Models can reveal problems which have not shown up in drawings. The next stage is to produce neat, detailed, **working drawings** as in diagram **C**.

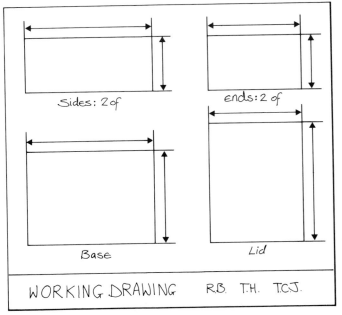

**C**  *Working drawing*

Planning work is important. Rushing into things usually leads to wasted time and, often, mistakes. It is particularly important when you are sharing equipment as in a school workshop. If there are 20 people all needing to use one drilling machine it is helpful if some have planned to use it one week and others the next week! In industry **production planners** make sure that there are no 'traffic jams' in a production line (see cartoon **D**).

**D**   The importance of planning

| Week | Plan |
|------|------|
| 1 | Gather materials, order hinges |
| 2 | Cut materials, mark out |
| 3 | Drill |
| 4 | Assemble |
| 5 | Etc. |

**E**   Work plan

Table E shows one style of work plan. Once all of the parts have been made and assembled, you are ready to **evaluate** your design. You need to answer questions like: does it do what it's supposed to, how well, how long will it last, can it be improved, how much did it cost and can you make it more cheaply so that it still works? Can you make it so that it looks nicer, so that more people will want one, etc? This stage of evaluation and testing may well show up problems that will need to be solved by defining exactly what the problem is, writing a specification, producing alternatives, selecting the best, planning it, making it and evaluating it. Problem-solving is a circular process.

## ▶ Things to do

▶ **1**   Copy the choice table (table **B**) and the work plan (table **E**).

▶ **2**   Look at diagram **D** and write five sentences about the importance of planning work.

▶ **3**   **Learn a skill – How to think about organising work**

An important aspect of factoring (making from parts) is everyone doing a bit of one job. Everyone must know his or her job and timing must be co-ordinated. You must have self-discipline and use initiative if there is a breakdown at any stage.

Imagine you have to make 100, ten page booklets from ten piles of pages from a printer (see diagram **F**). You have 20–30 potential workers in your class. Do you get the two nimblest workers to do it? One sorting and compiling, one stapling? Or is there a better way . . . well, why not try it?

▶ **4**   **Find a problem**   Find another classroom exercise like that in Task **3**. (Making Christmas cards?)

▶ **5**   **Solve a problem**   Design a system of tests to evaluate the effectiveness of a new design of school chair.

**F**   Coordinating jobs

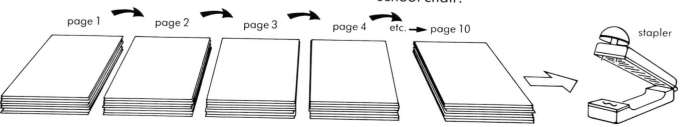

# 3.1 Wood

Trees grow in woods. Wood grows in trees. Wood is expensive – it costs money. You could say that money grows on trees.

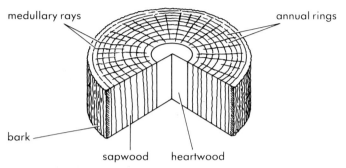

**A** Section of a tree trunk

The bark of a tree protects it from weather and pests and keeps it moist. Inside the bark are the living cells of the tree. The cells near the outside are young and have lots of 'give'. They are the soft sapwood cells. The cells near the inside are hard and tough. They form the strong heartwood of the tree (see diagram **A**). The wood near the heartwood is what the timber merchant is interested in. It is the wood used in furniture and in the building industry for planks, joints and rafters. Cartoon **B** shows how timber merchants get wood from trees.

It is not often that one piece of wood is used to make a complete article. Usually some form of jointing is necessary. Diagram **C** shows some common wood joining techniques.

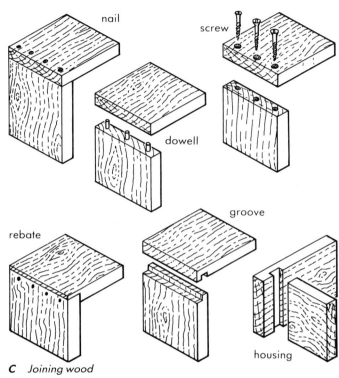

**C** Joining wood

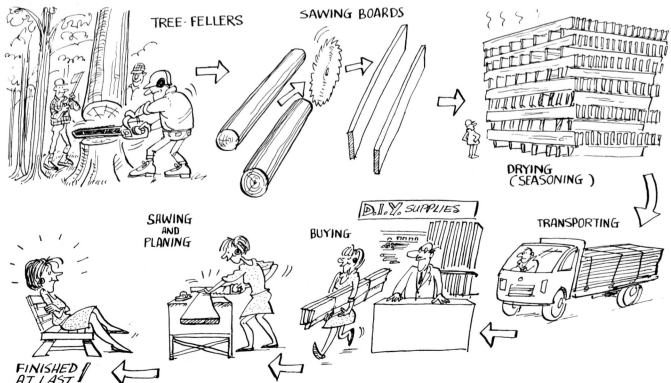

**B** Getting wood from trees

Wood is a very widely used material. It has been used throughout history. It is used because it is easy to cut and shape, it looks and feels good and is readily available. Trees can be replanted so wood is a **renewable** resource.

There are some problems in using wood:
1 It rots!
2 Woodworm!
3 It is **hygroscopic**. (That means it absorbs water and swells and warps.)
4 Its properties are irregular. Grain and knots make it difficult to work and to predict its strength.

Trees need these things to grow:
1 Water, from soil through roots.
2 Minerals, from soil through roots.
3 Carbon dioxide, from air.
4 Sunlight.

Sunlight converts carbon dioxide and water to glucose by *photosynthesis*. Glucose and mineral salts are then converted to cellulose which forms the walls of strong cells as the tree grows. Other minerals combine with cellulose to form a substance called lignin which gives wood its strength.

Technologists use many wood products – not only wood. Diagram **D** shows some of these.

## ▶ Things to do

▶ 1 Copy cartoon **B** to remind you how wood is turned into furniture.

▶ 2 Match the 'heads' to the 'tails' and write the complete sentences.

| HEADS | TAILS |
|---|---|
| a Young cells near the bark | is a renewable resource. |
| b The cells near the | are called sapwood cells. |
| c Wood | means that it absorbs water. |
| d Wood is hygroscopic, which | includes fruit, rubber and paper. |
| e Produce from trees | inside are hard, tough, heartwood cells. |

▶ 3 **Learn a skill – How to explain the advantages and disadvantages of wood as a constructional material**
   a Read through the sections on wood as a material and its problems.
   b List five advantages of wood.
   c List five disadvantages of wood.

▶ 4 **Think of a problem**   What in your house would benefit from or needs replacing with something of wood? Describe the problem and give details of the colour, strength and heaviness of the wood required to make what is needed.

▶ 5 **Solve a problem**   Design a machine which will take whole trees in at one end and through various bits and pieces (which you have to design!) will deliver planks, oils and charcoal at the other. Use your imagination!

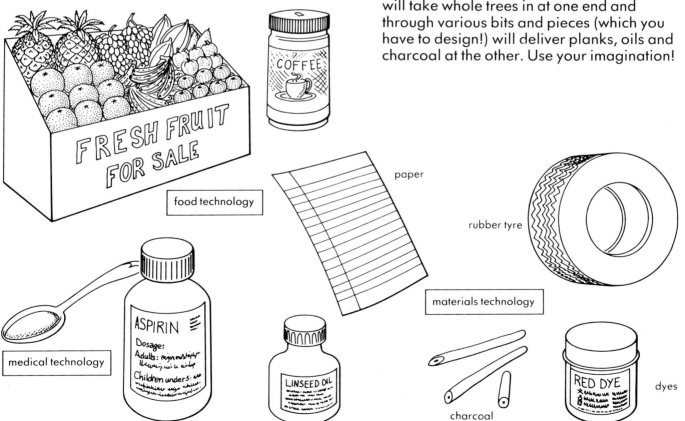

food technology

paper

rubber tyre

materials technology

medical technology

charcoal

dyes

*D   Other tree products*

# 3.2  Types of wood

There are two main types of wood; firstly natural timber and secondly, manufactured boards.

## Natural timber

Many different types of trees grow in many different countries and climates. Only a few are used in schools and industry. They have to be plentiful and must provide the right type of wood for the job in hand. There are two main types of natural timber: **hardwoods** and **softwoods**. See diagram **A**.

Hardwoods come from short, fat trees which grow slowly in rainy climates. In cool areas hardwoods have large, broad leaves and are **deciduous** (lose their leaves in winter) (see diagram **B**). Examples are:

> **Oak** – strong, attractive, hard-wearing wood used for quality furniture and cabinets.
> **Ash** – tough, flexible, used for handles of tools and ladders.
> **Beech** – close grain, very hard, used for workshop benches, toys and chairs.
> **Elm** – durable, used for garden furniture and coffins!

In tropical areas hardwood trees lose their old leaves and grow new ones throughout the year, so they are always green. Their wood is dark in colour. Three examples are:

Hardwoods used in furniture and decorative work
{ **Mahogany** – dark red.
**Teak** – dark brown.
**Ebony** – black.

Softwoods come from tall, thin trees which grow quickly in cold dry climates and have needle shaped leaves. They are **evergreen** (keep their leaves in winter) and bear seeds in cones, so they can be called **coniferous** (see diagram **C**). Examples are:

> **Pine** – honey-coloured, from Scandinavia and USSR, easy to work, cheap, used in home building (floorboards, beams etc).
> **Parana pine** – Brazilian softwood used for general 'joinery'.
> **Spruce** – resists splitting, used for 'whitewood' furniture.
> **Cedar** – long grain, weather resistant softwood used in garden sheds and panels.

Odd one out – **tropical balsa wood** – used for making model aircraft. (Although tropical woods are usually hard, this hardwood is very soft and very light.)

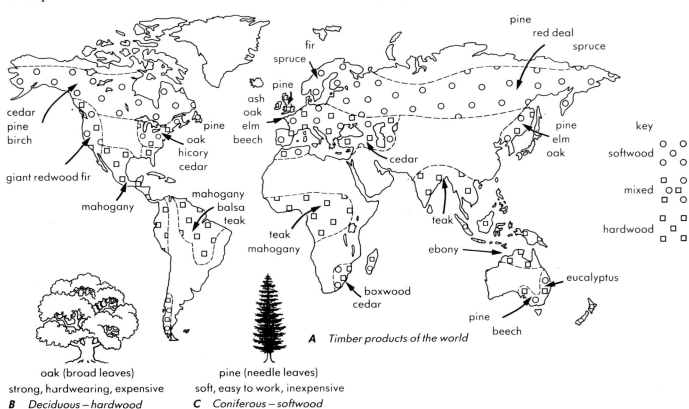

**A**  Timber products of the world

oak (broad leaves)
strong, hardwearing, expensive
**B**  Deciduous – hardwood

pine (needle leaves)
soft, easy to work, inexpensive
**C**  Coniferous – softwood

## Manufactured board

One problem with solid timber is that it is expensive. It also tends to warp, especially if you are using wide boards. To make wood cheaper and warpless, people have invented ways of combining woods into 'board'. Some manufactured boards are made from waste wood. Others use thin layers called **veneers** glued together to form **plies** of solid wood. Examples are:

**Plywood** – thin veneers glued together with the grain running at right angles in alternate layers. 3, 5, 7 or 9 ply are available. Strong, used in doors and drawers.

**Hardboard** – waste wood from branches to factory scrap. Chipped, pulped and compressed with resin to give cheap, thin board which may be textured, smooth, moulded or pegboard. Used as a cladding material.

**Chipboard** – wood chips glued and compressed to give cheap, brittle board usually covered with wood or polymer veneer, used in cheap furniture.

**Blockboard** – similar to plywood but middle 'ply' is strips of wood glued together faced with veneer. Strong, used in shelves.

Diagram **D** shows these boards.

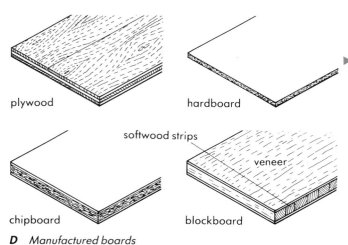

plywood

hardboard

softwood strips

veneer

chipboard

blockboard

**D** *Manufactured boards*

## Selecting timber

These are typical uses of common timbers.

Garden seat – elm.
Garden shed – cedar.
Wheelbarrow – elm.
Kitchen table – veneered blockboard.
Coffee table – mahogany.
Kitchen stool – beech.
Stepladder – pine.
Children's toys – beech.

## ▶ *Things to do*

▶ **1** Copy diagram **A**. Technology is important throughout the world and you need to be aware of where we get the raw materials for technology.

▶ **2** Rewrite these mixed up sentences so they make sense.
  **a** Plywood glued layers together is made from.
  **b** Hardboard is waste made from wood resin compressed with.
  **c** Chipboard chips wood is glued usually veneered is together and.
  **d** Blockboard plywood is similar but to middle ply of wood strips is the made.
  **e** Plywood, chipboard, blackboard, hardboard and all are boards manufactured.

▶ **3** **Learn a skill – Telling the difference between hardwoods and softwoods**
  Read the sections on hardwoods and softwoods. Look carefully at diagrams **B** and **C**.
  **a** Make a list of 5 differences between hardwoods and softwoods.
  **b** Make a list of 4 hardwoods and 4 softwoods and what they are used for.
  **c** Look at sketch **E(i)** (which shows trees) and sketch **E(ii)** (which shows finished timber products). Say which is softwood and which is hardwood, and give reasons.

▶ **4** **Find a problem** Design something which uses hardwearing hardwood, structured softwood or marvellous manufactured boards. All three materials *must* be used appropriately. Make detailed notes and drawings of your design.

**E(i)** *Trees*

**E(ii)** *Products*

# 3.3  Plastics

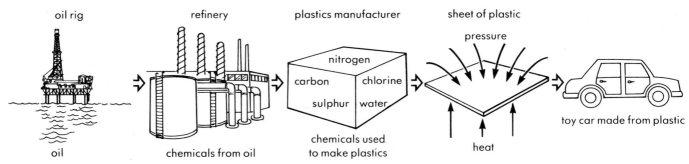

**A**  Making pastics

## What are plastics?

Plastics are generally synthetic materials. There are a few natural plastics but most are made from chemicals which are obtained from oil. When they are heated they become soft and can be pressed into shape (like plasticine!). The technical word for this property is 'plasticity'. Many plastics become 'plastic' when they are heated, that is why they are called plastics! Most plastics have carbon in them and are organic materials. Diagram **A** shows how plastics are made.

## Why are plastics used?

The problem with wood and metal is that they rot and rust. Plastics do neither which is why they are useful. They are chemical and weather resistant. They are also light, easy to mould, strong and come in a variety of colours. The paint may flake off metal and wood but the colour will not flake out of plastic! Plastics are used because they are so easy and cheap to shape, they look good and last well. Diagram **B** may help you remember some of the advantages of plastics.

## What types of plastics are there?

Diagram **C** shows some of the types of plastics and the types of things that are made from plastics. This list shows the chemical names for some common plastics and their more familiar names:

| | |
|---|---|
| polyethylene | polythene |
| polytetrafluorethene | PTFE |
| polyvinyl chloride | PVC |
| acrylonitrilebutadienestyrene | ABS |
| polymethylmethacrylate | acrylic |

Some plastics have very complicated chemical names! Many plastics start with the short word 'poly'. Technologists call plastics **polymers**.

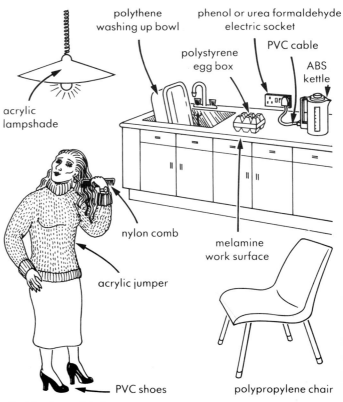

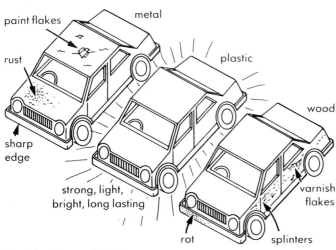

**B**  Advantages of plastics

**C**  Plastics and their uses

## What is a polymer?

Everything in the world is made of very small bits called **atoms**. Several atoms can join together to form **molecules**. Molecules are very small particles. Plastics are made from long chains of molecules joined together chemically. The scientific name for long chains of molecules is **polymer**. 'Poly' means many. 'Mer' means part. Polymer means many parts. (Polygon means my parrot has died!) Diagram **D** shows how a polymer is formed.

Several single molecules of styrene can be joined together in a process called **polymerisation** to form a long chain molecule of polystyrene. Lots of vinyl chlorides join together to form polyvinyl chloride (PVC) and so on.

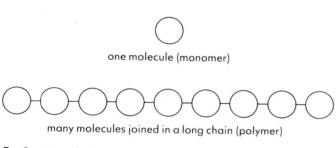

one molecule (monomer)

many molecules joined in a long chain (polymer)

**D** Structure of polymers

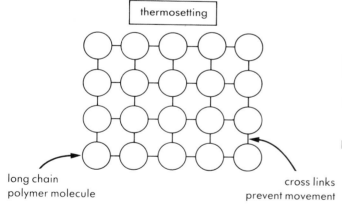

thermosetting

long chain
polymer molecule

cross links
prevent movement

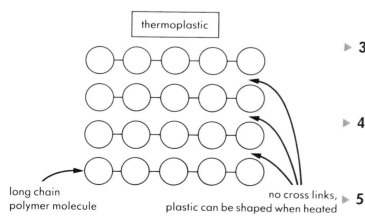

thermoplastic

long chain
polymer molecule

no cross links,
plastic can be shaped when heated

**E** Thermosetting plastics and thermoplastic plastics

## Two types of plastics

**Thermosetting** plastics are heated, moulded and set into shape. If they are reheated they do not soften because their long chain molecules are crosslinked. Most of the 'resin' plastics are thermosetting. **Thermoplastic** plastics soften when heated, can be shaped, harden when cooled and can be reshaped when reheated. The molecules in thermoplastic plastics are not linked but are free to move over one another. Polythene, acrylic and polystyrene are thermoplastics. Diagram **E** shows the difference between the molecules in thermosetting plastics and thermoplastic plastics.

## A problem with plastics

Plastics are used because they do not rot or rust but there is a problem. This is the **disposal** of plastics. If you throw an apple core away it disappears as it is eaten by birds or insects. A paper bag will rot, as will waste wood. Unwanted cars will (eventually) rust away. Plastics do not disappear when they are thrown away, most are not **biodegradable**. They cannot be burned safely as many of the fumes are poisonous and pollute the air. There is a problem in the disposal of plastics! Can you come up with a solution?

## ▶ *Things to do*

▶ 1 Copy diagram **A** which shows how we obtain plastics.

▶ 2 Write two or three sentences to explain each of the following:
   **a** plasticity,
   **b** polymer,
   **c** thermoset,
   **d** thermoplastic,
   **e** polymerisation.

▶ 3 **Learn a skill – To be able to identify the applications of the more common plastics**
   Study diagram **C** and make a list of common plastics and their uses.

▶ 4 **Think of a problem**   Write a short article for a newspaper to explain the advantages and disadvantages of wood, metal and plastic for making children's toys.

▶ 5 **Solve a problem**   Design a device to solve the problem of the safe disposal of unwanted plastic articles.

# 3.4 Metals

Can you touch a piece of metal near you now? A nail, screw, table leg, or radiator? What is a metal *like*? Why do we use it? Is it because it is hard, shiny, rings when hit, is long-lasting and strong? Think about some of the important properties of metals. Diagram **A** may help you.

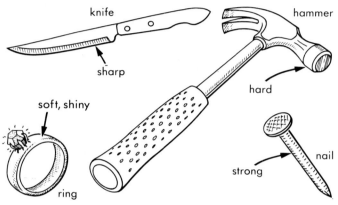

knife
hammer
sharp
hard
soft, shiny
strong
nail
ring

**A**   *Properties of metals*

Since Stone Age people first discovered gold and copper and started to move towards the Iron Age, the strength and ease with which metals can be shaped have made them important materials. The small pieces of gold and copper that were found were probably used for decorative work. Later, it was found that copper could be extracted from the mixture of minerals, rocks and dirt that is copper **ore**. This meant that lots of copper could be used and copper saucepans and spears started to appear for sale in 'Ye Olde Supermarkets' (see Cartoon **B**). Diagram **C** shows some of the important dates in the history of metals.

WOW! I'VE GOTTA HAVE ONE OF THOSE!

SHIRLEY'S DEREK GOT ONE LAST WEEK — HE SAYS THEY'RE FANTASTIC! — THEY'VE HAD STEAK EVERY NIGHT SINCE!

YE OLDE SUPERMARKET

COPPER POTS

STAYS SHARPER! LOOKS BETTER!

SPECIAL PROMOTION

METAL SPEARS!

YOUR OLD STONE SPEAR ACCEPTED IN PART-EXCHANGE!

**B**   *The Iron Age*

| | 10000 BC | 6000 BC | 3000 BC | 1000 BC | 1700 | 1886 | 1913 |
|---|---|---|---|---|---|---|---|
| **BRITAIN** | STONE AGE | | | BRONZE / IRON AGE | ZINC SMELTED | ALUMINIUM | STAINLESS STEEL |
| **MIDDLE EAST** | STONE AGE | COPPER AGE | BRONZE AGE | IRON AGE | ZINC SMELTED | ALUMINIUM | STAINLESS STEEL |

**C**   *History of using metals*

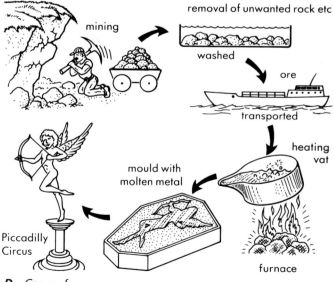

mining
removal of unwanted rock etc
washed
ore
transported
heating vat
mould with molten metal
Piccadilly Circus
furnace

**D**   *Copper from ore*

How do we get copper from ore? Well, first dig up the ore. This is called **mining**. Wash it to remove **gangue** (earth, rocks, etc). This should now leave you with comparatively pure ore. Now **transport** it to **furnaces**. Heat the ore, and the copper flows out (see diagram **D**). This is called **smelting** – (not melting, smelting!). Copper smelts at about

800 °C. Iron (which was discovered about 2000 years later than copper) is smelted at a much higher temperature (about 1600 °C). Iron ore is iron oxide and when it is heated on its own the iron will not smelt out. Carbon has to be around to separate the oxygen from the iron. Carbon is used as a **reducing agent**. Iron is smelted in a furnace which uses a blast of air. Diagram **E** shows a **blast furnace**. Economic (money!!!) and chemical technology problems have to be solved when extracting metals. Cartoon **F** shows some questions that have to be answered.

The answers to these questions will depend on how scarce and valuable the metal is. For gold it is economical to dig up one tonne of earth to get a few grams of the metal. Iron is so plentiful that mining technologists are really only interested if they can extract 250 kilograms of iron from each tonne of earth.

Ease of extracton of metal from ore also affects these decisions. Aluminium is the most plentiful material in the earth's crust. The problem is that aluminium silicate cannot be reduced cheaply yet. So, we get most of our aluminium from aluminium oxide (bauxite) which is scarcer but easier to reduce. Aluminium is extracted from the aluminium oxide ore electrically. One problem with this is that the electricity used to obtain one tonne of aluminium would be enough to light a light bulb for seven years. Electricity is expensive and so aluminium is expensive.

**F**   To extract or not to extract?

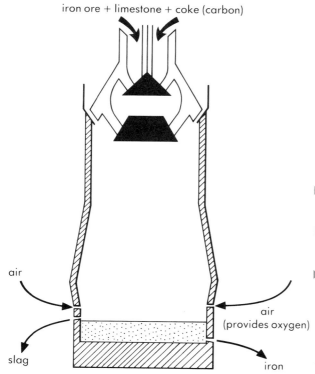

**E**   A blast furnace

## Things to do

▶ **1**   Copy the time chart in diagram **C**.

▶ **2**   Match the processes to the description and write them out correctly.

| Process | Description |
| --- | --- |
| **a** Mining | removes dirt and rock to leave ore. |
| **b** Washing | from mine to furnace is often by ship. |
| **c** Transportation | agents like carbon are sometimes used. |
| **d** Smelting | is the removal of ore from the ground. |
| **e** Reducing | is the process of removing metal from ore. |

▶ **3**   **Learn a skill – How to label a diagram**
Copy diagram **E** with appropriate labels.

▶ **4**   **Think of a problem**   Design a portable mining, washing and smelting plant.

▶ **5**   **Solve a problem**   Study cartoon **F** carefully. Describe who might find the answers to each question and how. For example, how much ore is there? Surveying technologists could identify possible sites by aerial surveys. After analysis of the photographs sample drillings would be done and the samples analysed by geological technologists. The results. . .

# 4.1　Types of metals

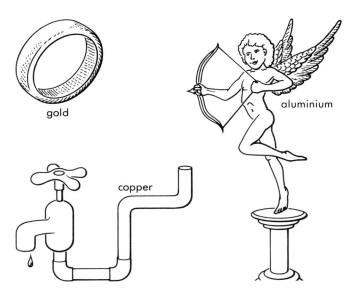

**A**　*Pure metals*

**B**　*Making alloys*

Some metals can be used in their pure state e.g. copper, gold, aluminium and silver (see cartoon **A**). More often metals are mixed with other metals to form a mixture called an **alloy** (see cartoon **B**).

Copper does not rust but is a bit soft for most uses. Copper and zinc form the alloy **brass**. Brass is harder than copper and is used in electrical components, taps and waste pipe fittings. Lead and tin form the alloy **solder** which is stronger than lead and melts at a lower temperature. Aluminium alloys have the light weight of aluminium but have higher strength than pure aluminium.

**Aluminium** – light, soft, white metal. Does not rust. Usually used as an alloy in windows, 'tin cans', saucepans, and in aircraft.
**Brass** – hardwearing alloy of copper and zinc. Yellow. Does not rust. Used in electrical components, brass doorknockers and taps.
**Copper** – reddish brown. Malleable (can be beaten into shape). Does not rust. Good conductor of heat and electricity. Used in electrical wire and central heating systems.
**Bronze** – alloy of copper and tin. Hardwearing. Used in springs and bell castings.
**Lead** – very soft, heavy, malleable, non-magnetic. Used in batteries, radiation shielding and as an alloy in solder.
**Tin** – soft. Does not rust. Most often used as a thin coating on steel. Tin plated steel is used in 'tin cans'. Lead and tin alloyed form solder.

The metals in this list contain no **iron**. They are called **non-ferrous**. The list which follows is of metals which contain iron. They are all called **ferrous** metals.

**Iron** – ductile (can be drawn out into a thread or wire) but not very strong metal which is usually used as the basis for iron alloys.
**Steel** – alloy of **iron** and **carbon**. Mild steel has about 0.3% carbon, high-carbon steel about 0.8%. Higher carbon content steels are harder but less ductile than lower carbon content steels. Stainless steel has 1% carbon, 8% nickel and 18% chromium (this helps it resist corrosion).
**Cast iron** – iron and 3%–4% carbon. Harder, more brittle than steel, used in castings.

The properties of metals can be changed in other ways apart from alloying. If a piece of steel is heated until it is red hot and plunged into cold water it will become harder (although it will become more brittle and more likely to snap). If the same piece of steel was heated and allowed to cool slowly it would be tougher and less brittle.

Heating and rapid cooling is called **quenching** (this hardens the metal). Heating and slow cooling is called **annealing** (this softens the metal). Both processes are examples of **heat treatment**. Hard metals may be brittle. Reheating to a lower temperature and slower cooling (in oil for example) will produce a steel which is hard and tough. This is known as **tempering** (see cartoon **C**).

**C** Heat treatment

# Things to do

**1** Put a heading 'Non-ferrous metals' and copy out the list of non-ferrous metals. Add any more that you (or your friends) can think of and find in any books. Put another heading 'Ferrous metals' and do the same for these.

**2** Match the property to the metal in diagram **D** and redraw each with its correct caption.

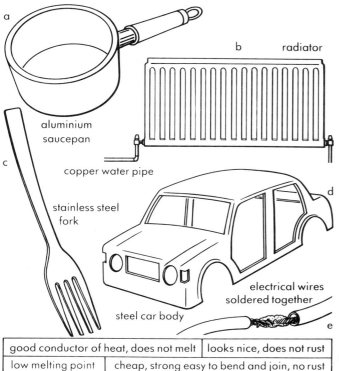

| good conductor of heat, does not melt | looks nice, does not rust |
| low melting point | cheap, strong easy to bend and join, no rust |

**D** Properties of metals

▶ **3** **Learn a skill – Identifying metals**
You will need:
**a** This book!
**b** Skills of observation, interpretation and common sense.

These things would be useful:
**a** Magnifying glass.
**b** Magnet.

Go around the room in which you are working. Examine in detail all of the objects which are made of metal (door hinges, window frames, radiator valves, desk legs etc). Use your experience and the information in this unit to decide which type of metal is used for each. Record your observations in a table like table **E**.

| Object | Metal | Observations |
|--------|-------|--------------|
| Desk leg | Mild steel | Painted black, magnetic, ... |

**E** Observations table

▶ **4** **Think of a problem** Look around the room you are in. Find an object which is *not* made of metal. Redesign it so that it could be made entirely of metal. Specify which metals you would use and why.

▶ **5** **Solve a problem** Design a device for use in a scrap yard to sort a mixture of metals into appropriate bins.

# 4.2  Shaping plastics

Plastics can be shaped into very complex forms by many techniques. Diagram **A** shows some of the ways in which plastics are shaped.

When choosing a way of shaping plastics the technologist needs to be aware of costs. The cost of machinery is low for hand lay up but high for injection moulding. Labour costs are high for hand lay up but low for extrusion. Moulds for vacuum forming are cheap but for injection moulding they are very expensive. To calculate the total cost is a complicated business. If you have a long production run or intend to make thousands of items then expensive equipment which works quickly may be economical.

| material | process | application |
|---|---|---|
| thermosets –<br><br>polyester resin | hand lay-up (with glass fibre) | GRP boat<br><br>formula one cars |
| thermosets –<br><br>phenolic (phenol formaldehyde)<br>UF (urea formaldehyde)<br>MF (melamine formaldehyde)<br>thermoplastic –<br>PVC (polyvinyl chloride) | powdered · heater · mould<br>compression moulding | phenolic handle<br>aluminium saucepan<br>UF plug<br>MF cup<br>PVC records |

*A*  Shaping plastics

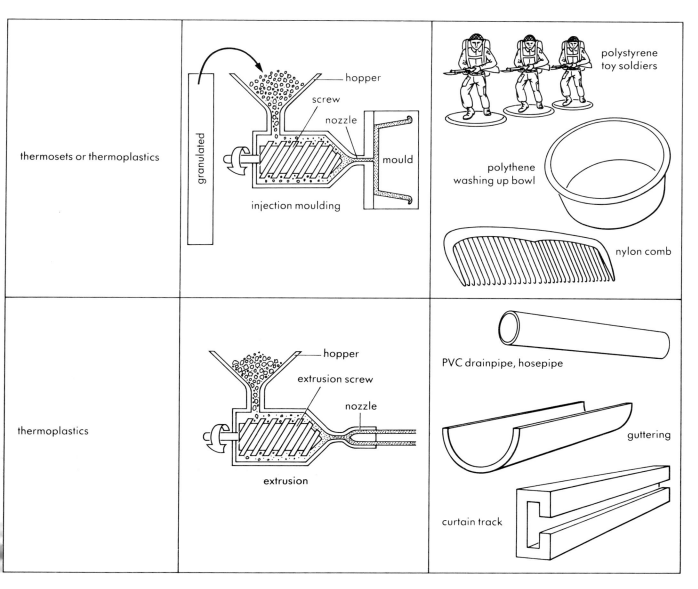

**A** *Shaping plastics (continued)*

# Things to do

1 Carefully make an exact copy of the diagram which shows the way in which polyester resin is shaped for a boat or a car.

2 Make a table like table **B**.

| Process | Application |
|---------|-------------|
| Hand lay up | Boats, cars, etc |

**B** *Complete the table*

Complete the table with processes and applications from this unit. Add extra applications if you can.

▶ 3 **Learn a skill – Identifying plastics shaping techniques**
   a Make a list of, say, 20 different types of things made from plastics.
   b Write alongside each the processes by which it is formed.

▶ 4 **Think of a problem** Think of items made from plastics which could not be made by the methods shown here. How are they made? (e.g. acrylic jumpers, PVC tablecloths, etc).

▶ 5 **Solve a problem** Design a mould to make an injection moulded cup with a handle. The one shown in the diagram will not work! Try to think of several different handle shapes and draw detailed drawings of the moulds for each.

# 4.3 Shaping metals

Diagrams **A** to **F** show some of the main ways in which metals can be shaped.

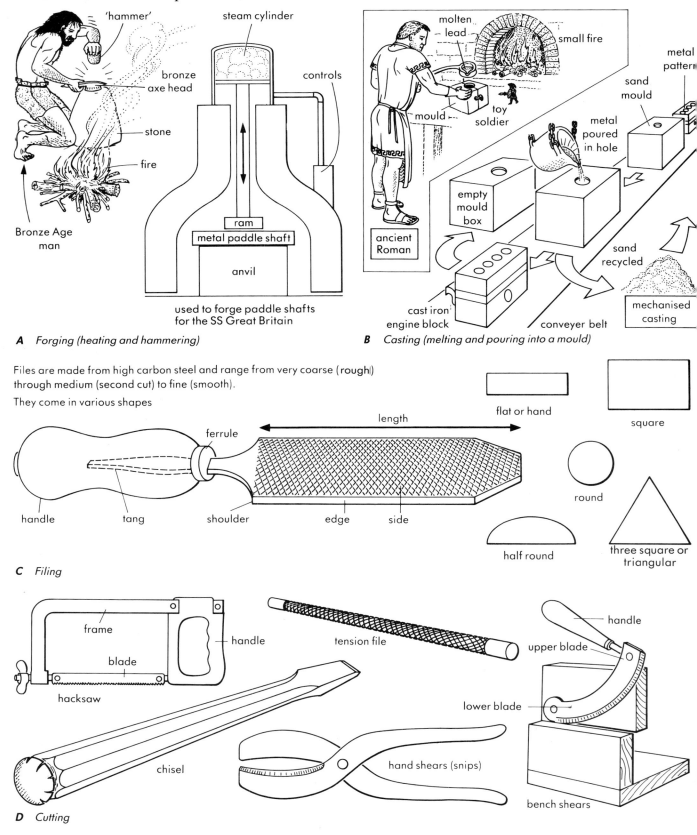

**A** *Forging (heating and hammering)*

used to forge paddle shafts for the SS Great Britain

**B** *Casting (melting and pouring into a mould)*

Files are made from high carbon steel and range from very coarse (rough) through medium (second cut) to fine (smooth).

They come in various shapes

**C** *Filing*

**D** *Cutting*

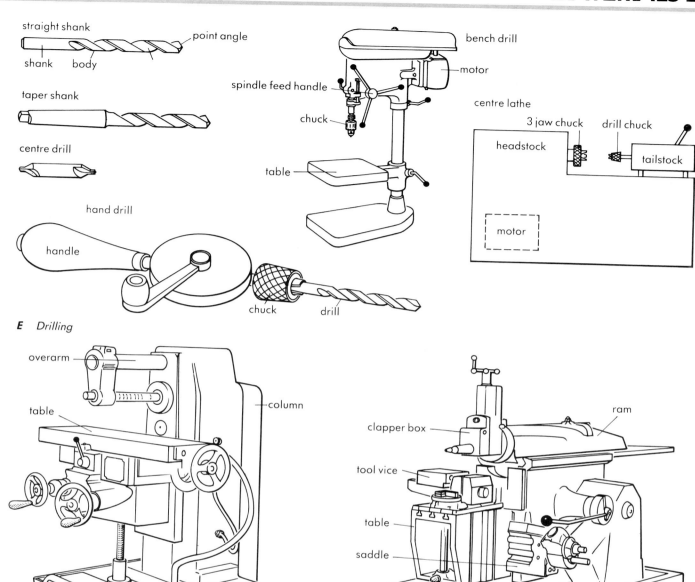

straight shank

shank  body  point angle

taper shank

centre drill

hand drill

handle

chuck  drill

bench drill

motor

spindle feed handle

chuck

table

centre lathe

3 jaw chuck  drill chuck

headstock

tailstock

motor

*E*  *Drilling*

overarm

table

column

milling machine

clapper box

tool vice

table

saddle

ram

shaping machine

*F*  *Machine tools (the lathe in diagram E is also a machine tool)*

## Things to do

**1** Carefully copy the drawings of the three types of drills (straight shank, taper shank and centre drill) and the three 'machines' used to turn these drills (hand drill, bench drill and centre lathe).

**2** Put six headings: 'Forging', 'Casting', 'Filing', 'Cutting', 'Drilling' and 'Working with Machine Tools'. Write one sentence to describe what you think is the most important thing about each activity.

**3** **Learn a skill – Finding out and doing** Choose the shaping method which your teacher says you can do in the classroom/

workshop about which you know *least*. Find out as much as you can about it. Try other classroom textbooks, or the school library, or ask a classmate, or (if desperate) ask the teacher! Then have a go at it. Good luck!

**4** **Think of a problem**   A trophy is to be presented to the 'Metalworker of the Year'. The trophy *must* be shaped using each of the shaping processes in this unit. What do you think it should look like? Use a diagram to show it.

33

# 4.4 'Other' materials

Woods, metals and plastics are by no means the only materials available to technologists.

**Glass** – Heating silica and potash to 1500 °C produces glass. Glass is very hard but extremely brittle. Safety glass is made by heat treating the glass to toughen it or by laminating glass with plastic. Diagram **A** shows some uses of glass.

**A** *Some uses of glass*

**Ceramics** – Porcelain, china and clay are used for pottery, kitchenware and, increasingly, as electrical insulators. The heat shields on spacecraft are ceramic. A high melting point and resistance to corrosion makes ceramics very useful. (See diagram **B** for uses of ceramics.)

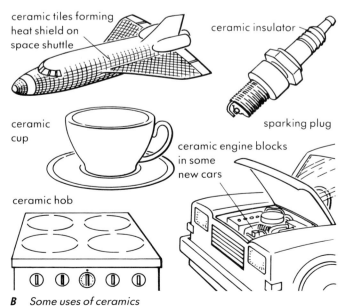

**B** *Some uses of ceramics*

**Cotton/wool** – Natural materials which are used for clothing, blankets etc (as are acrylics, nylon and polyester). The cotton industry was one of the first to be mechanised during the Industrial Revolution.

**Leather** – mainly used in boot and shoe manufacture. (See diagram **C**.)

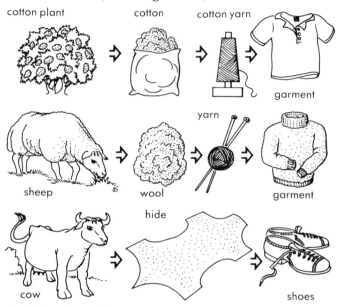

**C** *Natural materials*

**Cement** – Portland cement contains chalk and clay. Mixing cement, chippings and water produces concrete. Concrete is very strong in compression but weak in tension and is often reinforced with steel bars to improve its tensile strength (see diagram **D**).

**Semiconductors** – Silicon and germanium can be treated with impurities so that they will act as conductors or insulators of electricity. They are called semiconductors and are used to make electronic components such as diodes, transistors and chips. Using semiconductors, changes in heat and light can be converted into electrical signals (useful in fire alarms!).

**Asbestos** – a group of minerals which can be separated into fibres. Fire-resistant and heat-resistant, asbestos does not rot. Used in corrugated sheets as a roofing material, also in brake and clutch linings. Do not inhale asbestos dust – it is a severe health hazard.

**Diamond** – pure crystalised carbon. The hardest known natural material. Used in cutting and grinding tools and for styluses in record players.

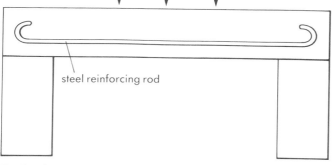

weak in tension

strong in compression

steel reinforcing rod

**D**  *Reinforced concrete*

## ▶ *Things to do*

▶ **1** Make an exact copy of the drawings in diagram **B** which shows the uses of ceramics.

▶ **2** Draw up a table with headings 'Material' and 'Application'.
List five materials and their uses. Do not include any metals, woods or plastics.

▶ **3** **Learn a skill – How to use and improve a key**
Study diagram **E**. Work through the key a few times, and try to improve it. (You will!) Then extend it to provide a key for all the materials found in this unit.

▶ **4** **Think of a problem**  Specify the properties which you want for a 'new' material. It could be for a space craft's heat shield or an idea of your own. Beware, do not ask the technologist to produce an unbreakable, unbendable, indestructable material which cannot be cut, drilled or shaped!

▶ **5** **Solve a problem**  Design a machine to 'un-knit' woolly jumpers so that the wool may be recycled.

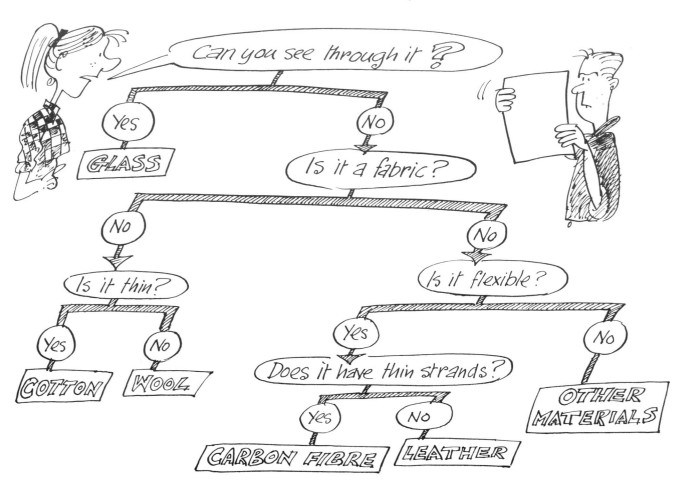

**E**  *Key*

35

# 5.1   What is energy?

The world relies on energy. Stone Age people used heat energy to keep warm and to keep animals away at night. Their fires also provided light energy to illuminate their caves. Modern technologists use many types of energy. Heat energy is used in engines, light energy in laser technology, nuclear energy in electricity generation, sound energy in communications systems, and so on. Transport especially relies on many different types of energy (see photographs **A**).

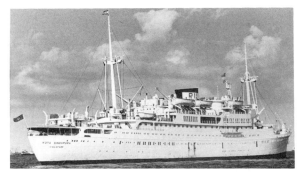

***A***   *Energy for transport*

There are many different types of energy used in many different places. Photographs **B** show some types of energy. But exactly what is **energy**? Well, energy is often used in making things work.

***B(iii)*** *Biochemical energy*

***B(iv)*** *Stored chemical energy*

***B(i)***   *Stored chemical energy*

***B(ii)***   *Nuclear energy*

***B***   *Types of energy*

***B(v)***   *Kinetic energy*

When you eat your toast and cornflakes in the morning your body changes the chemical energy into muscle (biochemical) energy. This energy is **potential** or stored energy waiting to be used. If you push a car you change your stored potential energy into energy of movement, **kinetic** energy. **Work** is done when a force moves something. According to the scientific definition, if you push, with all your energy, a car with its brakes on, but it doesn't move, you haven't done any work.

So where has your energy gone? The answer is that the energy has been changed from potential energy to heat energy – you sweat!

So now we can see that energy can be changed from one type to another and diagram **C** may remind you of some of these energy changes.

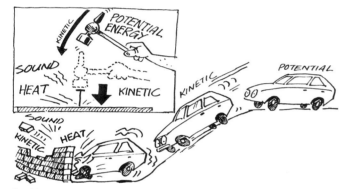

C    More energy changes

There are two basic laws of energy and these are very important to technologists. They are the energy equivalent of the Ten Commandments, they are the laws which cannot be broken. Cartoon **D** shows them.

D    The laws of energy

Common sense – energy makes things work.
Scientific sense – energy is the ability to do work.
Mathematical sense – work = force × distance moved.

Total work done is the same as energy used. Energy is measured in **joules**. **1 joule** of energy is used when **1 newton** of force is moved **1 metre**. The newton is named after Sir Isaac Newton and is roughly the force of a small apple pressing on a head. Any idea why?

Table **E** shows some energy changes.

| Energy change | Application |
|---|---|
| Mechanical to heat | Friction |
| Heat to mechanical | Engine |
| Electrical to heat | Electric fire |
| Heat to electrical | Thermocouple |
| Chemical to electrical | Battery |
| Electrical to chemical | Battery charger |
| Electrical to mechanical | Motor |
| Mechanical to electrical | Generator |
| Chemical to heat | Fossil fuel |
| Heat to chemical | Sunlight on plants |

E    Using energy changes

## Things to do

▶ 1    Copy diagram **C** to help you remember what energy and work are and how energy can be changed from one type to another.

▶ 2    When you hammer a piece of metal it gets hot. Write about the energy changes which take place. Chemical, biochemical, muscles, potential, kinetic, heat, sound are all words which you may find useful.

▶ 3    **Learn a skill – How to test a law**
Copy the two laws of energy in cartoon **D**. Choose one of them and explain how you would set about testing it.

▶ 4    **Think of a problem**    Electricity is so important as a source of energy that it is worthwhile to imagine what problems we would face if suddenly we were without it. Write entries in a diary to explain some of these problems, starting with the day electricity disappeared.

▶ 5    **Solve a problem**    Design and make a device to convert the kinetic energy of a rolling marble into sound energy. (You could build a simple helter-skelter from a cardboard tube and make the marble hit foil milk bottle tops as it rolls down, or you could be more inventive!)

# 5.2 Coal, oil and gas

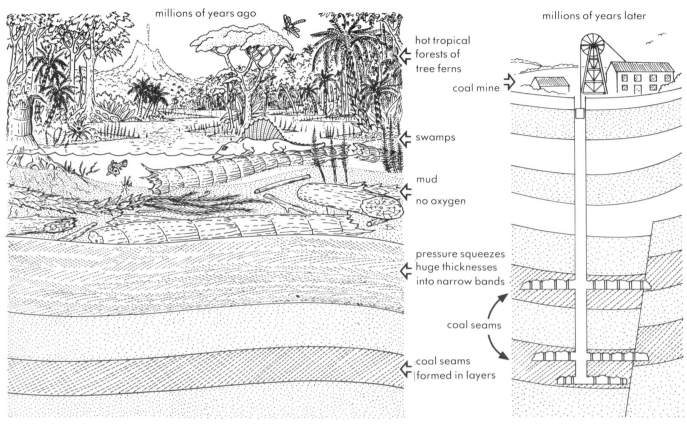

millions of years ago

hot tropical
forests of
tree ferns

coal mine

swamps

mud

no oxygen

pressure squeezes
huge thicknesses
into narrow bands

coal seams

coal seams
formed in layers

millions of years later

**A** *How coal was formed*

What is the source of your body's energy? What did you have for breakfast this morning? *Corn*flakes? *Wheat*abix? *Rice* krispies? All these came from cereals which we grow. Milk comes from cows which feed on grass. All need **sunlight** to grow, and so your energy comes from the **sun**.

All of our sources of energy come directly or indirectly from the sun. Solar energy usually means using sunlight directly to heat water in a solar panel or to make electricity using a solar cell. The connection between a lump of coal and the sun is less obvious. Coal, oil and gas are major sources of energy and all have what is called a 'solar origin'.

**Coal** was first used on a wide scale around 1600, when it became a popular domestic fuel, gradually replacing wood as a source of energy. Diagram **A** shows how coal is formed and that it has a solar origin. Diagram **B** shows how mining technology has changed.

**Oil** was used in 1870 to provide paraffin as a source of light energy. With the development of the internal combustion engine in 1900, oil became a very important source of energy

because it provided the petrol that the engine needed. Diagram **C** shows how oil (and gas which is formed at the same time) is formed.

Oil is often found where an ancient ocean no longer exists, e.g. in Saudi Arabia and Texas. Drilling methods vary depending on the area. There is only a certain amount of coal, oil and gas under the earth's surface. It has taken thousands of years to form and is replaced very, very slowly. Coal, oil and gas are **fossil fuels** – this means they are formed from ancient living organisms. They are also **capital** sources of energy – they are part of the energy which exists on the planet and when used will be gone forever. As there is a limit to how much exists, they are called **finite** resources.

How long the reserves of coal and oil will last is uncertain. It all depends on how much is used and the rate of new discoveries. Oil which is used as a heating fuel, as a transport fuel, to generate electricity and as a source of plastic would seem likely to run out within, say, 50 years. Coal reserves may be enough for, say, 1000 years.

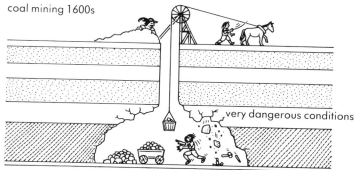
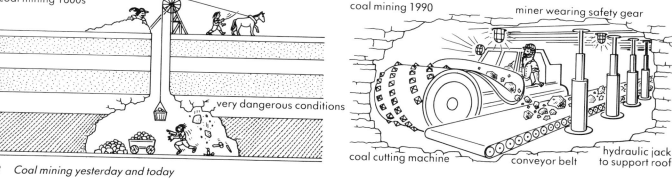

*B Coal mining yesterday and today*

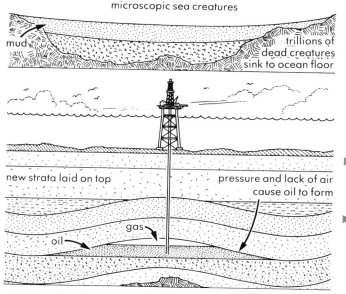

*C How oil and gas were formed*

## ▶ Things to do

▶ **1** Match the 'heads' to the 'tails' and write them out neatly.

**Heads**
a Our energy comes from
b Coal is formed
c Oil is used as a
d Coal and oil
e Capital sources of

**Tails**
from decayed vegetation.
energy are finite resources.
the sun.
heating fuel and transport fuel.
are both fossil fuels.

▶ **2** Draw a cartoon strip to show how coal, oil and gas are formed. Use diagrams **B** and **C** as a guide.

▶ **3** **Learn a skill – How to draw a working diagram**
A working diagram shows how something works. Diagram **D** shows an oil rig. Make a large (full page), clear, labelled working diagram of an oil rig, by adding these labels:

oil bearing rock
oil pipe up to the rig
oil pipe down to main pipeline
main seabed pipeline to shore
flare to burn off unused gas
supply vessel
helicopter pad
crew quarters
support leg

▶ **4** **Think of a problem**  Make a list of the advantages and disadvantages of coal, oil and gas as fuels for domestic heating. Think of a major problem with each.

▶ **5** **Solve a problem**  Imagine you are a politician responsible for making the reserves of coal, oil and gas last as long as possible. Write an 'Energy Policy' document and explain who you would send it to.

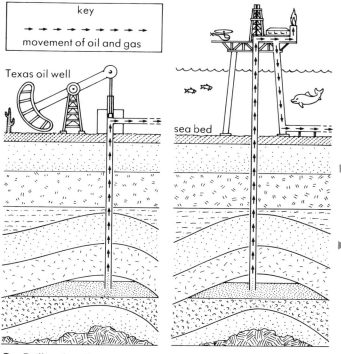

*D Drilling for oil*

# 5.3 Nuclear energy

Nuclear energy produces 10% of the world's electricity. All materials are made up of atoms and molecules. Nuclear energy uses the unstable atoms of **uranium** to produce energy. Diagram **A** shows the parts of an atom.

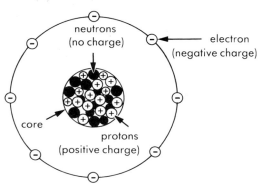

**A**  *Inside an atom*

In a uranium atom the neutrons tend to move around. As they move they can be made to collide with other atoms. This causes the atoms to split and form new atoms which releases more neutrons. This splitting of atoms and forming of new ones produces energy. Einstein discovered that the amount of energy could be calculated using the formula:

$$E = mc^2$$

where  $E$ = energy
$m$ = mass of atom
$c$ = speed of light

In a nuclear reactor this reaction takes place in a controlled way, with neutrons colliding with atoms in a **chain reaction** (see diagram **B**).

The vast amount of energy produced in this chain reaction from such small particles means that 1 kg of uranium can give the power to run an electric fire for 3000 years.

In a **nuclear reactor** rods of uranium are placed inside graphite blocks. The graphite **moderator** slows the neutrons down. The neutrons collide with the uranium atoms to create energy. **Control rods** of boron are used to absorb some neutrons to prevent overheating. See diagram **C**.

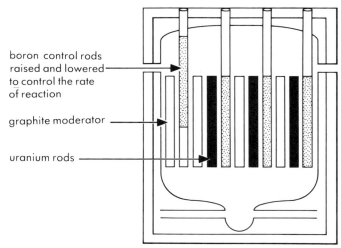

**C**  *A nuclear reactor*

To produce electricity the heat of this reaction is used to turn water to steam. **Carbon dioxide** gas is blown through the graphite. The heated carbon dioxide is passed over water tubes. The steam produced is used to turn a steam turbine. The turbine turns a generator and electricity is produced as in diagram **D**.

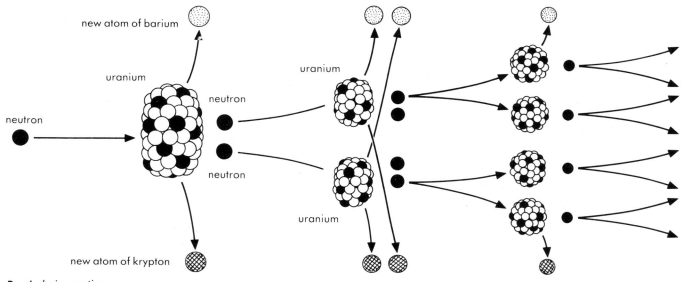

**B**  *A chain reaction*

40

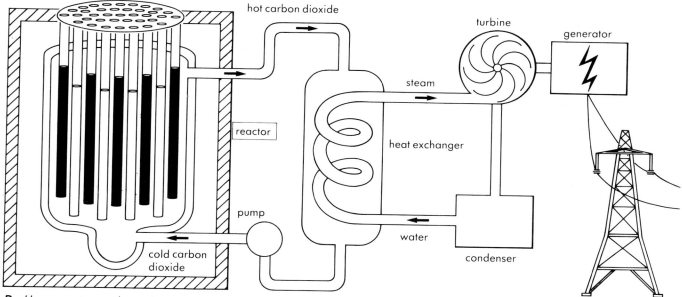

**D** How a reactor produces electricity

Splitting atoms is called **nuclear fission**. Energy can also be produced by joining atoms – **nuclear fusion**. Here hydrogen atoms are heated to the temperature of the sun – **100 million °C!** This makes the protons and electrons form **helium** plus **energy**. This process actually happens in the sun. As yet we can only produce these temperatures for a very short time – in, for example, the hydrogen bomb. The real problem for technologists is to produce and maintain this heat and to **control** the energy released.

**E** How would you reassure local residents?

## ▶ Things to do

▶ **1** **a** Copy the diagram of how electricity is produced in a nuclear power station (diagram **D**).
   **b** Write an explanation in the form of a chart to show what happens in this process.

▶ **2** Make notes with suitable diagrams to help explain **nuclear fission** and **nuclear fusion**.

▶ **3** **Learn a skill – Research a complex issue**
   Find out as much as you can about the nuclear accidents at Three Mile Island and Chernobyl. Write a short account of what happened, why, and with what effects.

▶ **4** **Think of a problem** What is the main problem with nuclear power? Imagine that there are plans to build a nuclear power station at the end of your street. Write a newsletter to your neighbours listing all the problems. The following headings may help you.
   Radioactive fallout
   Pollution
   Chernobyl
   Radioactivity lasts for thousands of years
   Terrorist target
   Waste disposal problem
   Do we really need it?
   Why not use solar power?

▶ **5** **Solve a problem** Imagine you are responsible for installing the power station in question **4**. Faced with the opposition of the residents, solve the problem! Explain what you would do to reassure the residents. Diagram **E** may give you some ideas.

# 5.4　The energy crisis

A　An energy crisis

| Year | World oil demand (millions of tonnes) |
|------|---------------------------------------|
| 1900 | 20 |
| 1920 | 100 |
| 1940 | 300 |
| 1960 | 1000 |
| 1980 | 3000 |
| 2000 | ???? |

B　Rise of the world oil demand

| Year | Oil prices ($ per barrel) |
|------|---------------------------|
| 1970 | 1.0 |
| 1971 | 1.3 |
| 1972 | 1.9 |
| 1973 | 3.1 |
| 1974 | 11.0 |
| 1979 | 14.0 |
| 1981 | 32.0 |

C　Rise of oil prices

Timber was a dominant source of energy until 1600 when the new growing cities had an *energy crisis* – there was a shortage of timber (see cartoon **A**). Coal was the alternative; the amount used in 1740 was 20 million tons/year – by 1900 it was 200 million tons/year (much of this was used to produce coke, which was a source of energy and a reducing agent in steelmaking).

From around 1900, oil was an increasingly important source of energy. Table **B** shows how the world oil demand rose rapidly. Drilling for oil was cheaper than mining coal. Oil (and gas) met the 20th century's increasing demand for energy. In 1970 oil prices rose sharply because:

1　oil discoveries fell,
2　oil demand was rising,
3　USA started to import oil,
4　petrol exporting countries formed the Organisation of Petroleum Exporting Countries (OPEC) which took control of prices.

Table **C** shows what happened to oil prices in a very short space of time. There was a new **energy crisis** and people started to look seriously at **alternative sources** of energy.

Coal leads to subsidence, accidents and pollutes the air with sulphur dioxide. Nuclear fuel has radioactive waste products. Most people mean non-polluting, natural sources of energy when they talk about **alternative sources of energy**.

Diagram **D** shows some of the alternatives which technologists and politicians are developing. The problem with these alternatives is that none of them is able to provide *all* of the energy we need. Most probably, in the future, coal and nuclear power stations will continue to be used as research goes on into the alternatives. Bit by bit the alternatives will supply small amounts of our total energy demand.

Some pioneers may run their homes on several sources of energy. Some small communities may be able to become **self-sufficient** in energy. They will not use any energy except what they can produce themselves. Diagram **E** shows how this could work. There is a problem with pollution from alternatives – not atmospheric pollution but **visual pollution** as diagram **F** indicates.

In order to make our supplies of coal, oil and gas last as long as possible, we need to **conserve** energy. **Insulating** our homes helps to conserve energy (and save money), see unit 6.4.

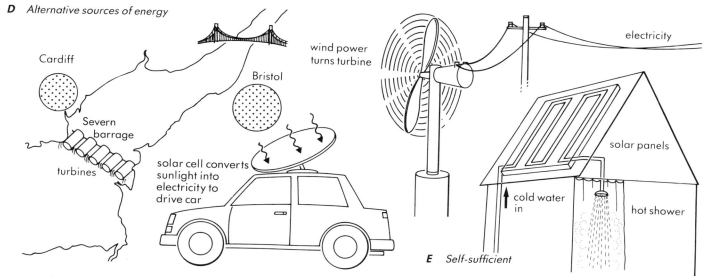

**D** *Alternative sources of energy*

Cardiff

Severn
barrage

turbines

wind power
turns turbine

Bristol

solar cell converts
sunlight into
electricity to
drive car

electricity

solar panels

cold water
in

hot shower

**E** *Self-sufficient*

**F** *Visual pollution*

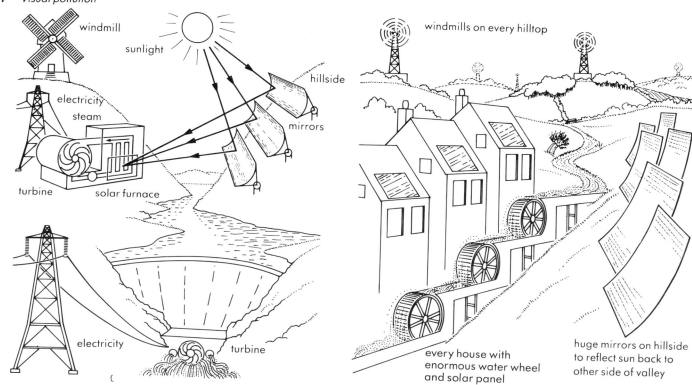

windmill

sunlight

hillside

electricity

steam

mirrors

turbine

solar furnace

electricity

turbine

windmills on every hilltop

every house with
enormous water wheel
and solar panel

huge mirrors on hillside
to reflect sun back to
other side of valley

# ▶ *Things to do*

▶ **1** Make a list of the reasons for oil becoming more expensive leading to the oil crisis in 1970–1980.

▶ **2** Draw up a table which will combine the information in tables **B** and **C** in one table. Give it an appropriate title.

▶ **3** **Learn a skill – How to 'empathise' with a problem of the past**
Imagine you are the mayor in cartoon **A**. The townspeople are calling for action. List the problems they face from the **timber shortage** (remember timber was used to build houses,

ships etc as well as being a fuel). List the alternatives that were available.

▶ **4** **Think of a problem** As energy becomes more expensive **transport** becomes an issue. The C5 designed by Clive Sinclair was an attempt to solve this problem. It failed to sell. Your problem is to find an area like this which will succeed and earn you a fortune.

▶ **5** **Solve a problem** Design an **alternative energy village**. Use some of the ideas in Diagram **E** and some of your own.

# 6.1 Solar energy

Solar energy is energy from the sun. The sun has been shining for 5000 million years, and it is likely to keep going for millions of years to come. Technologists are trying to find ways to put this energy to use.

Eastbourne, in the 'sunny south' of Britain, gets 1750 hours of sunshine in an average year. Graph **A** shows that May and June are its sunniest months. The sunniest places on earth are in the Eastern Sahara desert, which gets 4300 hours of sunshine per year. Deserts could form the energy stores of the future, if we can learn how.

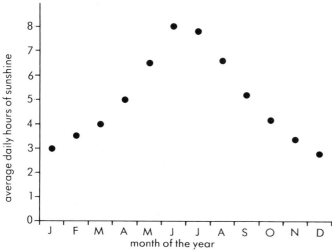

**A**  Sunshine hours at Eastbourne

We can use solar power in several ways:

## Photosynthesis

This means 'building with light'. Green plants take in light energy when they make food in their leaves. They give out this energy when they are burned as firewood, or when they slowly decay in compost heaps. But firewood and compost are too bulky for industrial energy production. It takes much more firewood than coal to produce the same amount of heat.

Some crops produce less bulky energy-rich materials. Sugar cane and water hyacinth are fast-growing 'energy crops'. The sugar from cane can cheaply be turned into alcohol, which can then be used instead of petrol in cars. Water hyacinths make the gas methane, which can be burned for energy. Three hundred tonnes of hyacinths can be grown per hectare per year. (One hundred tonnes of wheat would be a good crop from the same land.)

## Photoelectric cells

These are 'solar batteries' which turn sunlight energy into electricity. (See diagram **B**.) Calculators and watches can be solar powered, as are many parts of spacecraft. The problem at present, as diagram **C** shows, is that very large cells are needed.

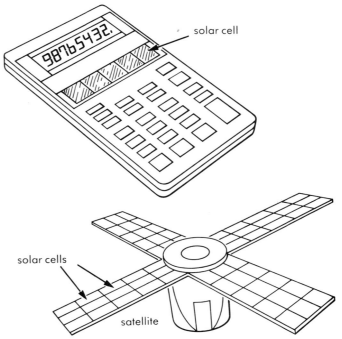

**B**  Solar powered

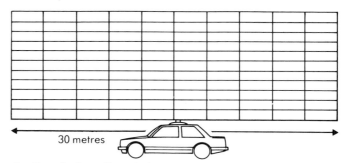

**C**  Size of solar cell needed to power a motor car

## Solar collection panels

These panels use sunlight to heat water. They are usually mounted on sunny south facing roofs. Diagram **D** shows the main parts of a solar panel. They can save 25–50% on water heating bills, even in British weather! But they are fairly expensive to make and fit. A sensor and valve are needed to make sure the water is not cooled when the sun goes in. Diagram **E** shows how solar panels fit into existing plumbing.

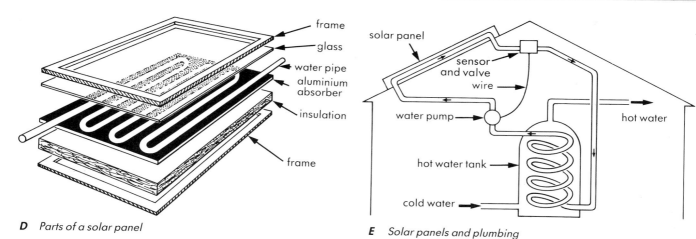

**D**  Parts of a solar panel

**E**  Solar panels and plumbing

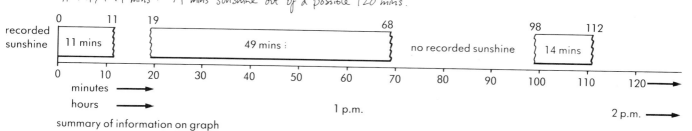

11 + 49 + 14 mins = 74 mins sunshine out of a possible 120 mins.

**F**  Sunshine recorded by eye from 12 noon to 2 p.m. at a school weather station 21 March 1987

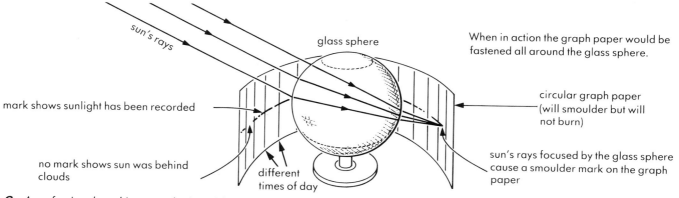

When in action the graph paper would be fastened all around the glass sphere.

**G**  A professional sunshine recorder (simplified)

# ▶ Things to do

▶ **1**  Copy diagrams **D** and **E** to show how solar panels work and how they are made.

▶ **2**  Write five sentences about each of the following:
  **a**  photosynthetic energy,
  **b**  photoelectric cells,
  **c**  solar panels.

▶ **3**  **Learn a skill – How to carry out a sunshine survey**
You can record sunshine by observing the sky and noting the time the sun shines between the clouds. Chart **F** shows how the results could be plotted. Two problems are that a) you have to keep watching and b) do you count faint sunshine through thin cloud? Diagram **G** shows how weather scientists record sunshine, without having to watch the sun the whole time. The sun has to be strong enough to mark the graph paper, so faint sunlight is not recorded.

▶ **4**  **Think of a problem**  Solar panels are used to reduce heating bills for owners of swimming pools. Think of another market for some form of solar energy. Draw up a poster to try to sell your idea to other people.

▶ **5**  **Solve a problem**  Design a form of transport which is powered by solar energy. Use the information in diagram **C** to help you.

# 6.2  Energy from water and wind

**A**  *The water cycle*

Have you heard of the water cycle? No, it's not a new type of transport. It is the way that we think about water moving from hills to the sea, from sea to air, from air to hills, and so on in a cycle. Diagram **A** shows that the wind plays an important part in the cycle, and that the energy to move water and wind in this way comes from the sun. Another cause of water movement is the spinning of the earth, plus the pull of the moon. These forces cause the ocean tides.

This movement energy can be changed into five types of power. They are **direct water power**, **hydroelectric power, wind power, wave power** and **tidal power**.

## Direct water power

If you have ever stood or swum in a river, you will have felt the strong force of the water on your body. 3000 years ago, someone invented a water paddle which could be turned by this force. The power could be moved onto land by an axle, as cartoon **B** shows. The power was used to turn stone wheels in a mill, for grinding corn into flour. The mill was called a 'Norse mill'. It generated about half of one horse power, similar to the power produced by the donkeys or people who used to do that job! In metric units, one horsepower is 746 watts.

**B**  *The water paddle*

## Hydroelectric power

Direct water power could not be used far from a stream until electricity was invented. Modern turbines produce 10 megawatts (1000 horse power) of electricity which can be moved along cables away from rivers to wherever it is needed.

Electricity produced by water power is called 'Hydro (water) – electric power'. The best sites are in mountains with high rainfall and well-fed rivers. Reservoirs are built to give a higher fall of water and to keep a store of water in case of dry spells. Sometimes it is worthwhile to use cheap night-time electricity to pump water back uphill into the reservoir. This gives stronger flow in the daytime, when demand is at its peak in homes and factories.

## Wind power

Windmills were used to grind corn from about 7 AD. Modern windmills generate electricity. They are used a lot in California in the USA, and could be built along the Atlantic coast of Britain.

The front cover of this book shows a windmill used for electricity generation situated near Gothenburg in Sweden.

## ▶ Things to do

▶ 1 Write a 200 word article on water power as if you are a technology reporter. You are allowed one diagram and one cartoon. You will find your problem is not what to put in – but what to leave out.

▶ 2 **Learn a skill – To develop an awareness of how technology should interact with the environment**
   a Copy diagram **C**. Study it carefully.
   b Discuss with your friends how the tidal barrage might affect:
      i tides in the upper part of the river,
      ii local wildlife, such as plants, fish, and wading birds,
      iii local people, such as anglers, tourists and travellers.
   c Write a paragraph for each point.

▶ 3 **Think of a problem**   You are an 'ideas group' in a technology research centre. Your boss wants your group to spot a problem which may affect any of the uses of moving water shown on this page. You might come up with a solution. Or even a new way of using the energy of moving water.
   a Think up some possible problems – no matter how far fetched.
   b Choose one of them – and find a solution to it.
   c As a group make a display showing the original use, the problem, and your group's solution.
   d Now go and have a look at all the other groups' displays.

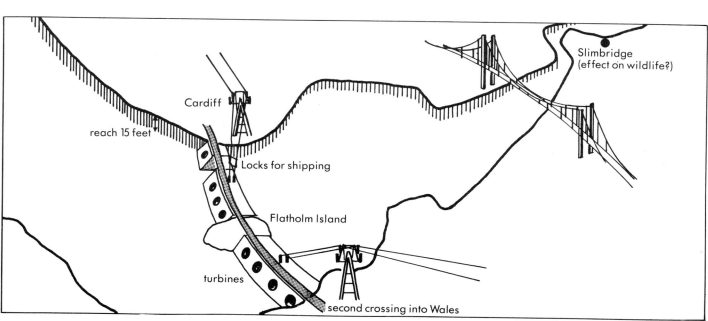

**C**   *New wave power*

# 6.3 Heat energy

**A** *Sources of heat*

Have you ever noticed that energetic sports players sweat? The water in sweat turns into a gas called water vapour. As it does so, it cools down the skin. This is the body's way of getting rid of unwanted heat. (See diagram **A**.) People have studied this link between heat, water and gas to make useful machines.

## The steam engine

If a small volume of water is heated enough, it turns into a large volume of steam. For example 1 cm³ of water starting at 10 °C turns into 100 cm³ of steam at 100 °C. If confined the steam pushes at the sides of its container with great force. This force can be used to work an engine. Steam power was used in Greek temples 2500 years ago. The great age of steam power was from 1750 to 1900. Steam engines were widely used to pump water out of coal mines. Later they were used for factories and transport. Photograph **B** shows a famous steam engine of that time.

**B** *George Stephenson's locomotive* Rocket

## The heat pump

These devices heat buildings by turning 'low grade heat' into 'high grade heat'. Anything that moves gives off low grade heat. It can be collected by passing a fluid near it in a pipe. The fluid absorbs the low grade heat. If the fluid is compressed, the heat is given off in a burst of high grade heat. Diagram **C** shows how a heat pump could work.

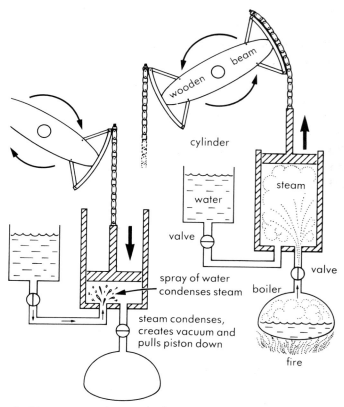

**C** *How steam engines worked*

A refrigerator is a sort of heat pump. It uses high grade heat to expand a fluid, which then cools rapidly. This cold fluid keeps the items in the refrigerator cool. (See diagram **D**.)

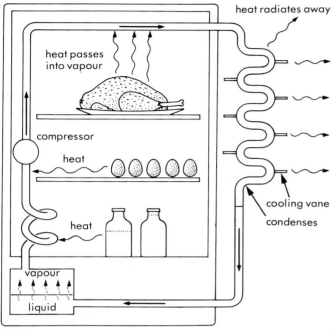

**D** A refrigerator – a reverse heat pump

## The internal combustion engine

'Internal combustion' means 'inside burning'. A fuel, such as petrol, is fed into a strong walled container and is ignited by a spark. It burns, forming gases with a much bigger volume, which push against the walls with great force, creating the engine's power.

Most modern cars are powered by engines which use the 'four stroke' cycle invented by Nikolaus Otto. Its working principle is shown in diagram E. Later a 'two stroke' engine was developed. Rudolf Diesel invented the diesel engine which is now used in most lorries. They all work on the internal combustion principle.

## ▶ Things to do

▶ **1** Copy diagram **E** which shows the four stroke engine cycle, sometimes called the Otto cycle.

▶ **2** Make your own notes on *steam power*.

▶ **3** **Learn a skill – How to calculate heat exchange efficiency**
If the heat given in to a heat pump is 100 watts and the heat given out is 50 watts, then 50/100 of the heat has been put to use.
As a percentage this is 50%.
$$\left(\frac{50}{100} \times 100 = 50\%\right)$$

We then say that the heat pump is 50% efficient. Now do these examples, **A**, **B** and **C**:

|  | A | B | C |
|---|---|---|---|
| Heat in | 25 watts | 50 watts | 1500 watts |
| Heat out | 50 watts | 200 watts | 6000 watts |

▶ **4** **Think of a problem** Think up a commercial market for a heat pump. First think of a situation where a heat pump would be a good idea. Then consider whether people would want to pay for the advantages of such a pump.

▶ **5** **Solve a problem** Thomas Newcomen invented an engine. A problem at the time was to make the valves open and close at the right time. It had to be done by hand. Can you think of a way of doing it automatically?

Each of you should draw an engine. In your group, discuss ways of solving the problem. When your group agrees on an idea, draw it up to make your own record.

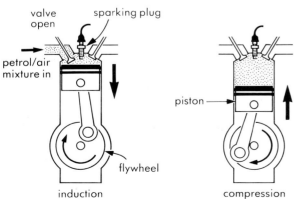
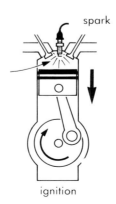
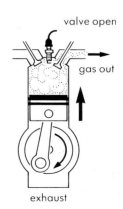

**E** The Otto cycle

# 6.4 Conserving energy

**A**   Conserving energy?

The lazy chap, Terry, in cartoon **A** is trying to conserve his energy. **Conserve** means use as little as possible. In fact, he is using a lot of energy. Electricity is needed to power his video system, coffee maker, light and sun lamp, and gas is being burned in his fire. In rich countries many of us are like Terry. We use a lot of energy. Diagram **B** shows some ways in which the use of energy is growing.

At times this leads to an energy shortage. We need to learn how to conserve energy so we can make the best use of it. One way is to keep our homes from losing their **heat**. Diagram **C** shows how heat can move from place to place.

**Heat loss by convection** can be kept low by closing and draughtproofing doors and windows, especially in winter. Buildings, like supermarkets, which have a lot of people coming and going can lose a lot of heat if doors are left open. This is why they often have doors which open and close automatically. Hot air rises, and 30% of a home's heat can be lost through the roof. A roof can be insulated (to keep the heat in) by laying layers of felt or glass fibre in the loft.

**Heat loss by conduction** can be kept low if insulation is added to the walls and windows of buildings. Walls are built with two skins of bricks with an **air cavity** in between them. If this cavity is filled with polyurethane foam, another 15% of the home's heat loss can be prevented. Ordinary windows allow heat to be conducted to the outside air. Double glazed windows cut down this heat loss. They have two panes of glass with a sealed air gap between them. This insulates the window against heat loss and also reduces noise passing into or out of the house. This is very useful if you live near a main road or airport, or if you like your radio on loud!

These methods also help cut down **heat loss by radiation**.

Another waste of energy happens if buildings are heated too much. A building can be kept at the right temperature by use of **thermostats**. They measure room temperature and control the heat given out by central heating boilers. This makes sure the room stays as warm as is needed.

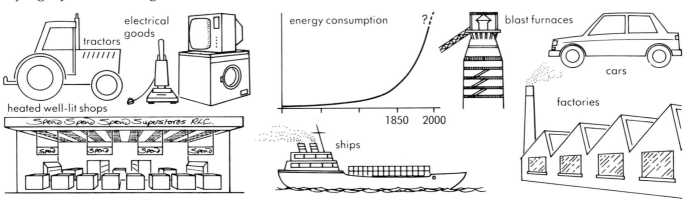

**B**   Increasing energy consumption

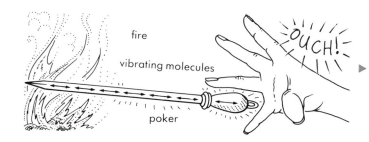

conduction

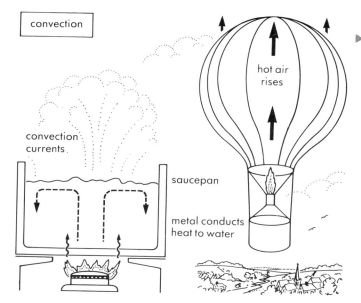

convection

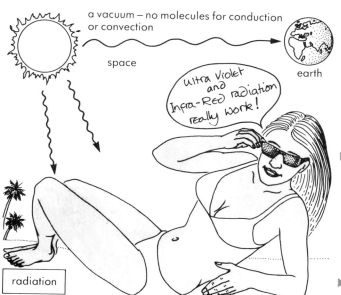

C   Conduction, convection and radiation

### ▶ Things to do

**▶ 1** Match the heads to the tails.

| Heads | Tails |
|---|---|
| **a** Conduction | reduces heat loss and saves energy. |
| **b** Convection | is how heat travels through a vacuum. |
| **c** Radiation | happens in gases and liquids. |
| **d** High energy | is heat movement from molecule to molecule in a solid. |
| **e** Insulation | use often comes with high living standards. |

**▶ 2** Write three or four sentences and draw a diagram to explain:
  **a** conduction,
  **b** convection,
  **c** radiation,
  **d** cavity wall insulation,
  **e** heat.

**▶ 3** **Learn a skill – How to insulate**
Vagrants who sleep in the open sometimes sleep in cardboard boxes wrapped in newspaper (see photograph **D**). Using a shoe box, one sheet of newspaper and one sheet of corrugated cardboard, design and make a model of an insulated home for a vagrant.

**D**   Insulation

**▶ 4** **Think of a problem**   Carry out an energy survey of your school. Note doors left open, windows which cannot be closed, areas of high heat loss, uninsulated areas, lights left on, radiators not working or not used. Find out the total energy bill for the school. Suggest ways to reduce this bill by 10%.

**▶ 5** **Solve a problem**   Houses without cavity walls cannot have cavity wall insulation. How could solid walls be insulated?

# 7.1 History of machines

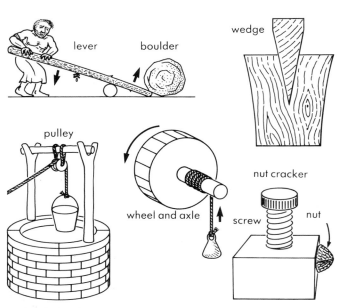

**A** Early machines

Five early machines are shown in diagram **A**. All helped extend human ability to lift and move things. Hero of Alexandria explained how and where these were used in 1 AD.

Rollers were also useful, particularly when used with, say, the wedge as cartoon **B** shows. Log rollers were eventually cut to make wheels which later were lightened and spoked. Later still, inflatable, shock absorbing tyres were fitted.

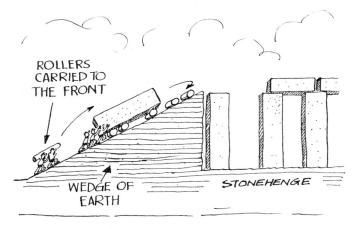

**B** Rollers and wedges

Ancient machines enabled the pyramids of Egypt and temples of Sumer to be built to a high standard of **engineering**. The Romans created military engineers who built seige machines – towers, ballista, etc (see cartoon **C**). As time went by machines were used to help build the Medieval churches, castles and towns which still last today.

**C** Roman military engines

All of these machines helped extend muscle power. Animal power made life even easier and photograph **D** shows an animal powered device. Later it was realised that natural forms of energy could be used and so engines were developed. First wind then water were used to power engines. Eventually fossil fuels were used in steam engines. Once steam had arrived on the scene, there was a versatile, powerful source of power ready to hand. As it arrived at the same time as good quality steel and improvements in engineering skills, more and more complex machines could be developed. Woollen mills were **mechanised** so that instead of being a long, slow and tedious process, weaving became very rapid and unskilled. Weavers' wages dropped from £5 to 50p per week between 1750 and 1850! Not surprisingly not everyone liked the new machines and there were frequent riots at mills. See cartoon **E**.

Farming noticed a particular change. It had been **labour intensive** employing lots of people (and animals) in ploughing, sowing, reaping etc. Machines made work easier but meant that there were fewer jobs.

Modern factories use computerised robot workers 'who' are accurate, untiring and can work in unhealthy conditions (see photograph **F**). Microprocessor control has made work so much easier that we now have a problem of too much free time – something that the Egyptians (or at least their slaves!) never found a problem.

**D**   A horse gin for raising coal from a mine

**E**   Mechanised mills

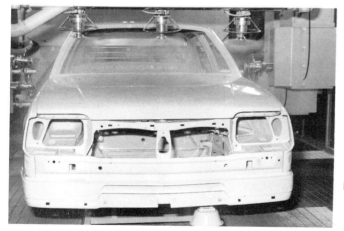

**F**   A robot worker painting a car

Some definitions:

**Machine** – a device which does work by transmitting or converting energy (e.g. bicycle, drill)

**Engine** – a machine which converts a natural form of energy into useful work (e.g. water wheel, car engine)

**Mechanism** – part of a machine (e.g. lever, gear)

## ▶ Things to do

▶ **1**   Draw the five early machines.

▶ **2**   **a** Write a short, illustrated, history of machines.
  **b** Draw five pictures to explain how machines have changed washday:
  i) Hand washing, ii) Washing tub, mangle, washing line, iii) early washing machine, separate spin dryer, iv) modern automatic washing machine and tumble dryer, v) the *future*!

▶ **3**   **Learn a skill – How to draw a machine**
Find a machine. Take off as many inspection panels etc as you can to reveal how it works. Make a neat, clearly labelled diagram of the machine.

▶ **4**   **Think of a problem**   Invent a manual process that would be better mechanised or a mechanised process that would be better 'manualised' to create more work.

▶ **5**   **Solve a problem**   Use Fischer-Technic, Meccano, Lego or bits of wood, string, sellotape etc to make a model drilling machine.

# 7.2 Levers

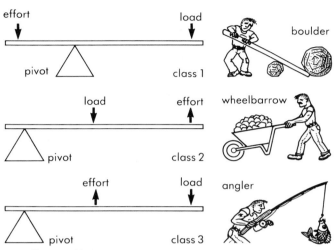

A  Classes of lever

Levers are probably the earliest types of machine. There are three main types of lever, diagram **A** shows these three **classes of lever**. These types are found in all sorts of everyday things as diagram **B** shows.

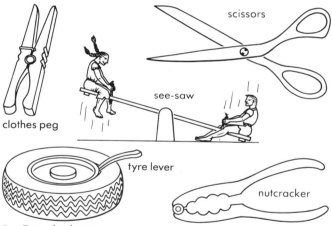

B  Everyday levers

Sometimes levers are used to increase the effect of an effort (diagram **C**). The advantage gained by using a lever is called the **mechanical advantage**.

$$\text{Mechanical advantage} = \frac{\text{LOAD}}{\text{EFFORT}}$$

So, if an effort of 1 newton is used to raise a load of 10 newtons

$$\text{the M.A.} = \frac{\text{load}}{\text{effort}}$$

$$= \frac{10 \text{ newtons}}{1 \text{ newton}}$$

$$\text{M.A.} = 10$$

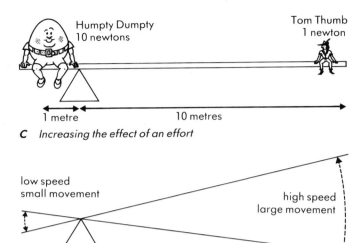

C  Increasing the effect of an effort

D  Amplifying speed and movement

As well as being used to give you a mechanical advantage, levers can be used to amplify either movement or speed as in diagram **D**. The ratio of the speed or velocity at each end of the lever can be calculated by the formula:

$$\text{Velocity ratio} = \frac{\text{DISTANCE EFFORT MOVES}}{\text{DISTANCE LOAD MOVES}}$$

## Turning force (torque)

The turning force (or torque) used by the spanner in diagram **E** can be calculated using the following formula:

$$\text{Torque} = \text{FORCE} \times \text{DISTANCE}$$

A longer spanner exerts more force than a shorter one.

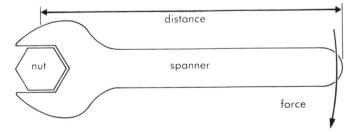

E  Turning force

A lever is really quite like a spanner when it comes to working out the turning effect of forces and if you look at diagram **C** you can work out the forces which are acting on each end of the lever. If the seesaw exactly balances then the force on one end must equal the force on the other. The turning force taking place is called a **moment**:

Moment = FORCE × DISTANCE

The moment which tries to make the lever turn clockwise (**the clockwise moment!**)

= 10 newtons × 1 metre

= 10 newton metres

**The anticlockwise moment**

= 1 newton × 10 metres

= 10 newton metres

The clockwise moment = the anticlockwise moment and so the seesaw balances.

Diagram **F** shows some more class 1 levers, where calculations of moments can tell you more about what is happening.

## ▶ Things to do

▶ **1** Copy diagram **A** which shows the three **classes of levers**.

▶ **2** i Copy diagram **B** and write alongside each whether it is a class 1, 2 or 3 lever.
ii Find other examples of levers, make simple drawings of them and label the pivot, load and effort positions.

▶ **3** **Learn a skill – How to calculate: mechanical advantage, velocity ratio, torque, moments.**

Copy the calculations in the text and then try the examples in diagrams **G** and **H**.

▶ **4** **Think of a problem** Find a daily task where a lever would be useful.

▶ **5** **Solve a problem** Design a strength testing machine to enable a lightweight arm wrestler to compete on equal terms with a heavyweight.

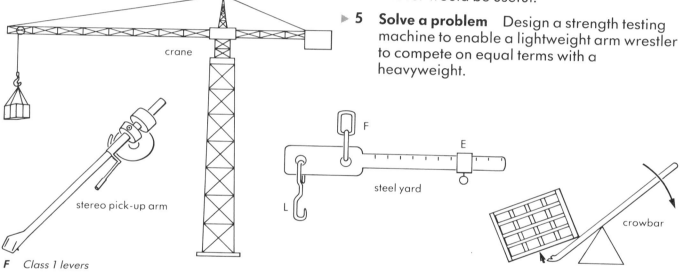

*F Class 1 levers*

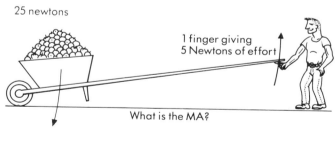

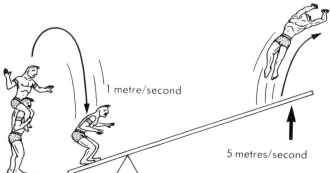

**G** Try these

**H** And these!

# 7.3 Pulleys and gears

## Pulley

A pulley is similar to a class 1 lever turning through 360° as diagram **A** shows.

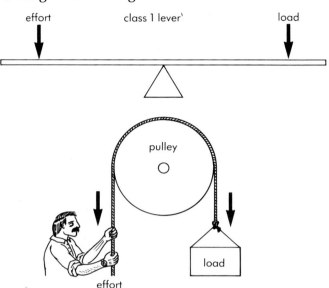

**A**   *Pulleys and levers*

Single pulleys can be fixed to a beam and used to hoist, say, an engine out of a car. Here the idea is to make lifting easier not by reducing the effort but by changing the direction of the effort. The mechanical advantage (load/effort, remember!) is 1 (see diagram **B**).

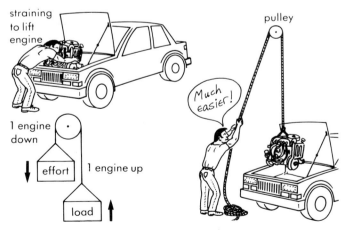

**B**   *Using a pulley to advantage*

Another way of using a single pulley is shown in diagram **C**. Here because the pulley is fixed to the load, the load moves a shorter distance (half the distance actually) than the effort moves. The load moves half the distance of the effort – the mechanical advantage is 2.

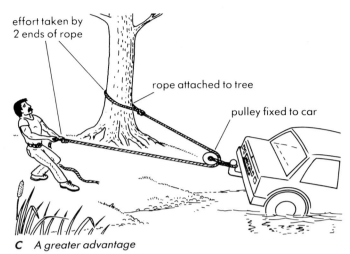

**C**   *A greater advantage*

Diagram **D** shows some arrangements which use multiple pulleys. The more pulleys you use, the less effort is required to move a given load.

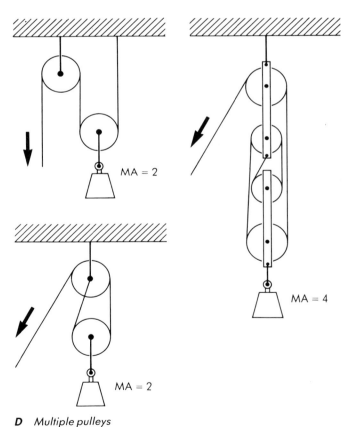

**D**   *Multiple pulleys*

## Wheel and axle

The wheel and axle (windlass) gives you a mechanical advantage by having a large diameter wheel on a small diameter axle. The effort is applied over the wheel which gives it greater leverage than the load exerts through the axle. See diagram **E**.

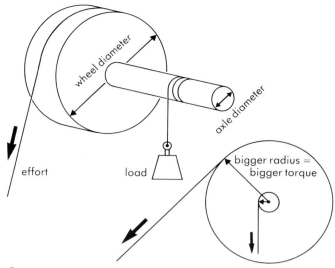

*E*    *Increasing and reducing speeds*

*effort*    *load*    bigger radius = bigger torque

Two gears with their **teeth in mesh** act like two levers (see diagram **F**) and can be used to vary speed or power. High speed gears give low power and low speed gears develop high power.

Gear ratio =

$$\frac{\text{NUMBER OF TEETH ON DRIVEN GEAR}}{\text{NUMBER OF TEETH ON DRIVER GEAR}}$$

The gears shown in diagram **F** are spur gears (because they look like cowboy's spurs!). Bevel gears are used when you want to change the direction of drive. A worm and worm wheel also allow a change in direction, as does a rack and pinion. Diagram **G** shows these three special gears.

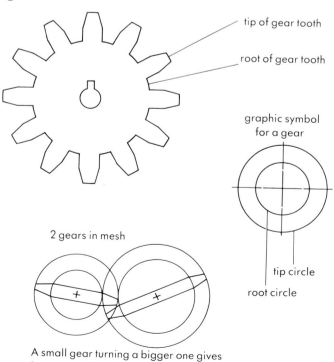

*tip of gear tooth*

*root of gear tooth*

*graphic symbol for a gear*

*tip circle*

*root circle*

*2 gears in mesh*

A small gear turning a bigger one gives lower speed but higher torque.

*F*    *Gears with teeth in mesh*

## ▶ *Things to do*

▶ **1**   Copy diagrams **A**, **E** and **G**.

▶ **2**   Write three sentences about each of the following:
   **a** pulley,
   **b** wheel and axle,
   **c** gears,
   **d** 'special' gears,
   **e** changing speeds.

▶ **3**   **Learn a skill – How to calculate gear ratios**
   Write this down:

   Gear ratio = $\dfrac{\text{Number of teeth on driven gear}}{\text{Number of teeth on driver gear}}$

   Invent five different sets of gears in mesh. Calculate the gear ratios.

▶ **4**   **Think of a problem**   Look at diagrams **B** and **C** to see how pulleys can be used to change direction of effort or reduce effort. Draw diagram **D** with each pulley set being used in different circumstances.

*bevel gears*

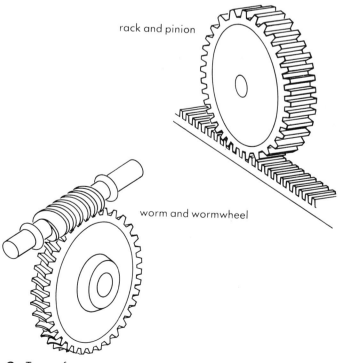

*rack and pinion*

*worm and wormwheel*

*G*    *Types of gears*

# 7.4 Mechanisms

Mechanisms change input movement or force into output movement or force. A pulley changes input force and movement which is downwards into upward movement in diagram **A**.

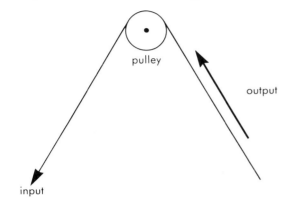

**A** Down becomes up

There are four basic types of motion:

**Linear** – straight line, you walking to school!
**Reciprocating** – straight line in one direction and then back along the same path. The needle on a sewing machine reciprocates.
**Rotation** – circular movement like the wheel on a bicycle.
**Oscillation** – circular reciprocation! Like a pendulum.

Diagram **B** shows these four types of motion.

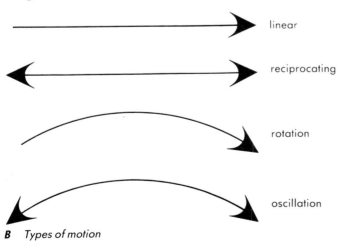

**B** Types of motion

**Black box** mechanisms are simplified diagrams that say 'I don't know anything about mechanisms, but I want something or other to change this type of movement into that'. A mechanisms technologist with a knowledge of levers, pulleys, gears and simple machines will be able to decide what goes inside the black box. Diagram **C** will illustrate the idea.

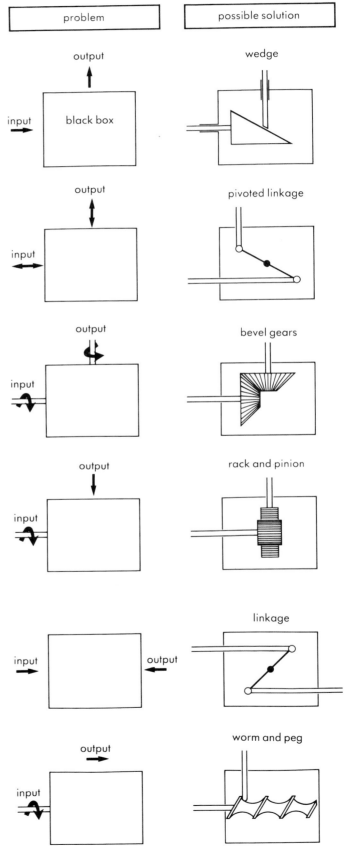

**C** Insides of black boxes

Black box problems and solutions shown in photographs **D** and **E** are two common mechanisms. Diagram **F** shows some more mechanisms.

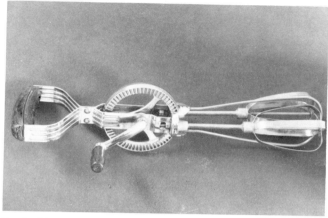

*D  Problems. . .*

*E  . . . and solutions*

## ▶ Things to do

▶ **1**  Copy diagram **B**. Write one sentence about each type of motion. Give one example of each in action.

▶ **2**  Copy the black box problems and solutions in diagram **C**. Give one application of each. Try to think of an alternative solution for each.

▶ **3**  **Learn a skill – How to solve a black box problem**
In a sewing machine rotational movement of the handwheel is changed into reciprocating movement of the needle and movement of a 'footplate' to move material forward.
**a**  Draw this as a black box problem.
**b**  Solve it!

▶ **4**  **Think of a problem**   A cam is a shaped piece of metal which changes the direction of movement. A ratchet is a set of teeth into which a pawl fits, to allow movement in one direction only. Find a problem where a cam and a ratchet would help provide the solution.

▶ **5**  **Solve a problem**   Draw the lathe in diagram **F** as a series of black box problems. This would be the first stage in creative thinking to design a new lathe without being guided too much by the existing solution. Design a simple lathe.

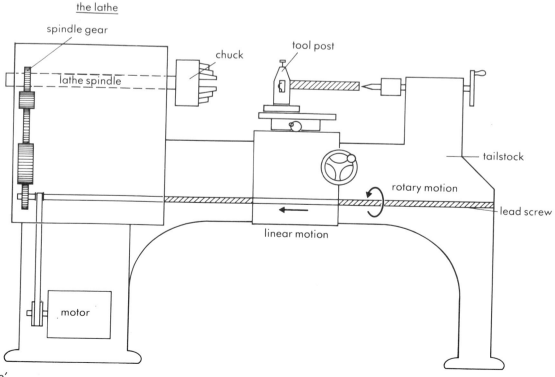

*F   'The lathe'*

# 8.1 Properties

Materials technologists have to know all about the materials that may be used by engineers. They help the engineer choose a material which has suitable **properties** (see cartoon **A**). Materials used in bridges must be strong and protected against corrosion. Medical equipment must be sharp and easily sterilised. Furniture must look good and be comfortable.

**A**   A materials technologist

## Appearance

Colour and texture is often important in the appearance of a product. Materials used in lamps, reflectors and mirrors must reflect light (light colours and metals reflect). A colour panel should absorb light (dark colours absorb). A window should be transparent (glass), a door may be transparent (toughened glass) or opaque (wood) depending on where it is used and why.

## Mechanical properties

**Strength** – resistance to pushing, pulling or twisting forces. A chair must be made of a material which resists the pushing (compression) force of you and the floor. A tug of war rope must resist the pulling (tension) force of the two teams. A key must resist twisting (torsion) forces. See cartoon **B**.

**Hardness** – resistance to scratching. Diamond is very hard – it will scratch most other materials. Glass-cutters, scribers, drills and floor tiles are all hard. See cartoon **C**.

**Toughness** – ability to absorb energy. Tough plastic bumpers on cars absorb the shock of impact, polythene mixing bowls are tougher than ceramic mixing bowls.

**B**   Compression, tension and torsion

**C**   Harder than diamond

**Ductility** – ability to be stretched. Car body panels are made from ductile steel which is stretched into shape in a hydraulic press.

**Elasticity** – ability to behave like an elastic band – to return to shape after being stretched or squashed. A guitar string is elastic (up to the point when it is overtightened, then it passes its elastic limit then breaks!). See cartoon **D**.

**D**   Elasticity and plasticity

**Plasticity** – ability to stay in new position after being stretched or squashed. Plasticine is plastic.

**Magnetism and electricity** – permanent magnets are used as compass needles. They will not point North if they are surrounded by steel components, they have to be shielded with non-magnetic materials. An electromagnet uses the fact that a magnetic field is formed when an electric current is passed through a wire. Electromagnets are used in scrap metal yards. Electricity will pass through some materials (**conductors**) but not through others (**insulators**). An electric plug has conducting pins in an insulating cover. Some materials are able to be conductors until conditions around them (such as heat or light) change and then they switch to being almost insulators. This is useful in electronics (see cartoon **E**). Transistors are made from silicon or germanium **semiconductors**.

SEMI-CONDUCTOR UNIT WHICH TURNS ROBOT ON WHEN IT DETECTS RAIN.

*E    Useful electronics*

## Thermal properties

Some materials **conduct** heat, others **insulate**. Ideally a saucepan should have a conducting pan and insulating handle. Aluminium and copper are good conductors. Wood and plastic are good insulators. When materials, especially metals, are heated they expand. Railway lines and road bridges are designed to allow for the difference in their length and width from summer to winter.

## Things to do

1   Copy diagrams **B**, **C** and **D** which will remind you of the forces on a material, and the difference between hardness and toughness, elasticity and plasticity.

2   Match the following property, 'middle bit', and use. Redraw the table. E.g. **a** Magnetic materials are used in loudspeakers.

| Property | 'Middle bit' | Use |
|---|---|---|
| **a** Magnetic | insulation is important | loudspeakers. |
| **b** Electrical | materials are used in | used in spectacles. |
| **c** Thermal | properties in structures | switches and plugs. |
| **d** Mechanical | properties affect the lenses | in houses. |
| **e** Optical | conductors are used in | affect how strong they are. |

▶ 3   **Learn a skill – How to use a key and how to build up a key to materials via their properties**

a   A key is a diagram which gives you different pathways for Yes and No answers. The pathways allow you to identify different things by asking questions about them. Study diagram **F** which shows a simple key to do with materials and their properties. It shows one way of identifying plasticine, balsa wood, steel and diamond.

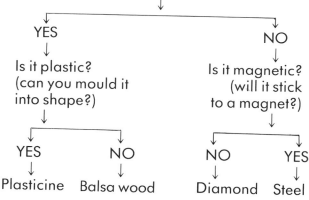

*F    Key*

Keys are useful because they allow non-experts to identify things easily.

b   Invent your own key to make different pathways for these materials: cement, glass, aluminium, hardboard. Use these properties: hard/soft, transparent/opaque, powder/solid.

▶ 4   **Think of a problem**   Look around the room you are in. Look at the different materials which are used. Why are they used? Find one area that is an obvious problem. Describe what the problems are and how they might be overcome.

▶ 5   **Solve a problem**   Suggest an alternative material to paper for use in schools. What properties should it have? What advantages should it have over paper? How can you correct mistakes? How much will it cost?

# 8.2 Joining materials

**A** How to join it?

**C** Soldering and welding

It is not often that you make anything from one piece of any material. Usually you will have to join several component parts together. Fixings or fastenings may be either **permanent** (like glue) or **temporary** (like nuts and bolts).

Before choosing your method of fastening you have to consider the materials to be joined (you can't weld wood!). Cartoon **A** shows some questions that have to be answered.

When choosing the actual method there are more questions as cartoon **A** also shows.

Now let's look at what is available to us. First, permanent fixings using adhesives (see photograph **B**).

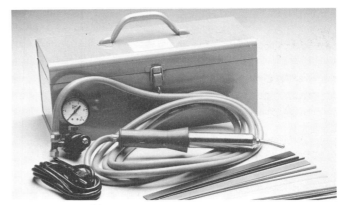

**C(i)** Plastic welder

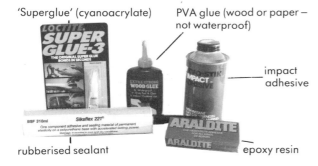

**B** Adhesives

**C(ii)** Arc welder

Soldering and welding are used with metals (although some thermoplastics may also be welded by heating). The photographs in **C** show some of the equipment used.

'Mechanical' fixings are methods of joining, using for example, nails and screws.

The final group of fixings is mechanical joining which does not necessarily use an adhesive or heat or third component. Diagram **D** shows some of these.

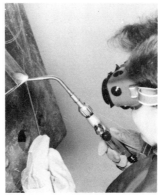

**C(iii)** Gas welder

**C(iv)** Soldering

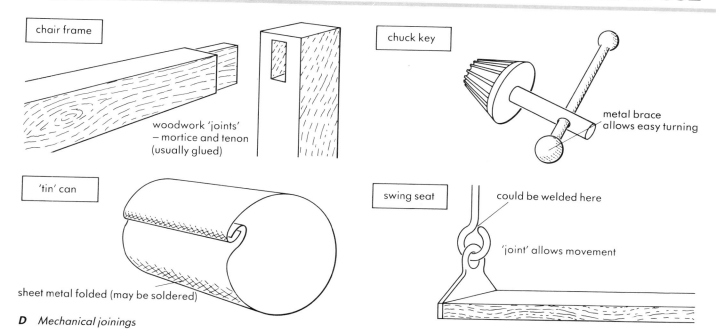

D   Mechanical joinings

# ▶ Things to do

▶ **1** Table **E** shows some common adhesives and their advantages and disadvantages. Copy it into your notebook or folder.

▶ **2** Make a half page drawing of a car. Label the various types of joining methods used. (Wheels and nuts, door hinges and bolts, windscreen and rubberised sealant. . . .)

▶ **3** **Learn a skill – Identify adhesives for a variety of uses**
Complete table **F**.

▶ **4** **Think of a problem** which uses as many of the joining methods mentioned in this unit as possible (and maybe some others!).

▶ **5** **Solve a problem** What type of joining would you use for the various problems encountered in installing aluminium double glazing? You would have to join metal to metal, metal to brick, metal to wood, make joints etc.

| Type | Preparation | Strength | Water resistance | Material |
|------|-------------|----------|------------------|----------|
| PVA (Resin W) | Ready to use | Good | Poor | Wood, paper |
| UF (Cascamite) | Mix with water | Very good | Very good | Wood |
| Impact (Evostik) | Ready to use | Good | Good | Wood, metal and plastic |
| Epoxy resin (Araldite) | Mix adhesive and hardener | Very good | Very good | Most materials |
| Acrylic (Tensol) | Ready to use | Fair | Fair | Acrylics |

E   Common adhesives

|  | Wood | Paper | Metal | Thermoplastic | Thermosetting | Fabric | Glass | Stone |
|--|------|-------|-------|---------------|---------------|--------|-------|-------|
| Wood | PVA | PVA | Araldite | | | | | |
| Paper | | | | | | | | |
| Metal | | | | | | | | |
| Thermoplastic | | | | | | | | |
| Thermosetting | | | | | | | | |
| Fabric | | | | | | | | |
| Glass | | | | | | | | |
| Stone | | | | | | | | |

F   Complete this table

# 8.3 Surface finishes

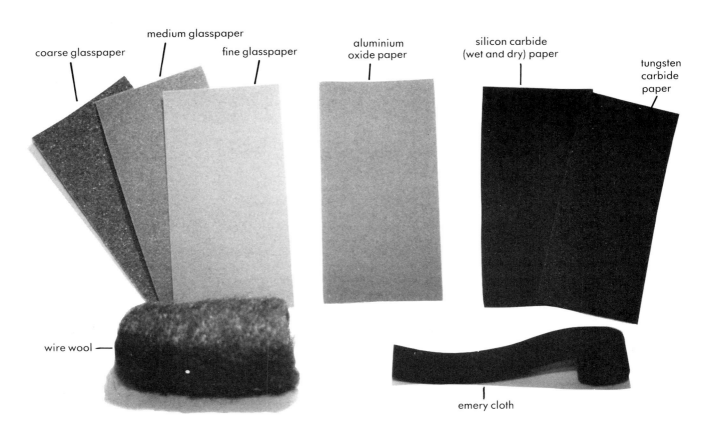

coarse glasspaper

medium glasspaper

fine glasspaper

aluminium oxide paper

silicon carbide (wet and dry) paper

tungsten carbide paper

wire wool

emery cloth

**A** *Abrasives*

**Abrasives** – The first stage in getting a good finish to your work is to use a fine abrasive to remove marks made by tools and machines in manufacture. Photograph **A** shows the following abrasives.

**Glasspaper** – usually crushed glass from bottles, does not last long and tends to clog easily. Available in several grades.

**Aluminium oxide** – used on commercial sanders, stays sharp and does not clog.

**Silicon carbide** – hard artificial abrasive often mounted on waterproof backing (wet and dry paper). Often used for rubbing down paintwork on cars, etc.

**Emery** – a mixture of corundum and magnetite on a cloth backing used on metals.

**Tungsten carbide** – particles mounted on metal backing, very long lasting.

**Wire wool** – used to clean up dirty metal, does not clog. Also used on timber between coats of varnish.

## Finishes

Finishes are used to:
   **a** improve appearance,
   **b** protect against water, dirt or grease.
Diagram **B** shows the difference between 'finished' and 'unfinished' materials.

rust

B160X    A10SD

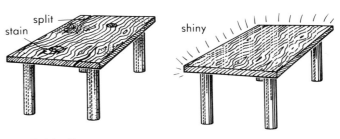

split

stain

shiny

**B** *Finished?*

**C** There is a wide variety of paints available

## Paint (see cartoon **C**).

Easy to use, wide range of colours, good protection. The method of use is:

1 Clean surface.
2 Use undercoat.
3 Lightly glasspaper.
4 Apply 'topcoat' of paint.
5 Add extra topcoat if necessary.
6 Clean brushes!

Polyurethane additives give improved resistance to wear.

### Woodstain
Water, oil or spirit-based stains can darken wood to match other (more expensive!) woods or to emphasise the natural grain.

### Wax polish
Brush on a thin layer on white polish, leave it to dry and then put on wax polish with a soft cloth. Polish to shine with clean cloth. Looks good but not very protective. Used on wooden furniture.

### Linseed oil
Used to reveal grain and preserve timber.

### Varnish
Hardwearing gloss or matt finish which protects wood but does not mask 'natural' appearance of grain. Polyurethane is added to improve wear, heat or abrasion resistance. Often used on boats.

### Creosote
Preserves wood used in fencing and so on. Obtained from coal tar, repels water but is dirty to apply (and smelly!). Only used on outside timber.

▶ **Things to do**

▶ 1 Copy the crossword solution in diagram **D**. Write your own clues for each answer.

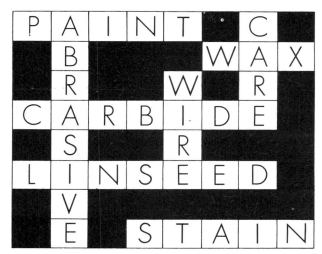

**D** Make up the clues

▶ 2 Rearrange these sentences so that they make sense.
   **a** remove the   tools and machines   Abrasives   marks of
   **b** crushed glass   Glasspaper is made   by gluing   onto paper
   **c** Wet and dry   made from   paper is   silicon carbide
   **d** abrasive is   A longlasting   metal backing   tungsten carbide   on a
   **e** dirty metal   Wire wool   cleaning up   is used for

▶ 3 **Learn a skill – Selecting the most appropriate surface finish**
   Which surface finishes are best for the following applications?
   **a** Oak coffee table
   **b** Pine kitchen table
   **c** Steel car body
   **d** Plywood dinghy
   **e** Pine children's toy
   **f** Cedar garden shed
   **g** Cricket bat
   **h** Decorative walnut cabinet
   **i** Door to 10 Downing Street!

▶ 4 **Think of a problem** Write a specification for a 'new' surface finish to be used on school desks.

▶ 5 **Solve a problem** Draw a sequence of pictures to be put on a paint tin to describe without words how the surface should be prepared, various layers applied and the brushes cleaned.

# 8.4    Friction and lubrication

The study of moving surfaces, friction, wear and lubrication is called **tribology**. A useful word to impress your friends with!

What is **friction**? Friction is the force which tends to stop two surfaces sliding over one another. The friction force between your shoe and the pavement is usually high, the force is lower between shoes and ice, and cartoon **A** shows the result!

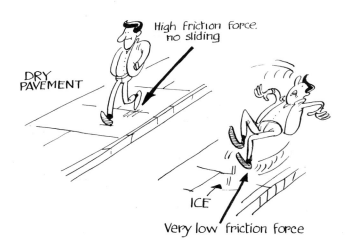

**A**    *Ice decreases friction*

On the positive side friction helps you to walk, makes the brakes on your bike work and it stops your notebook sliding all over the desk as you write! On the negative side friction can lead to heat and wear.

Friction depends on the:
1 materials used in the two surfaces (hard or soft),
2 surface finish (rough or smooth, wet or dry),
3 forces pushing surfaces together.
Cartoon **B** will remind you of these factors.

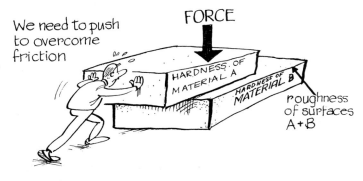

**B**    *Friction depends...*

## Lubrication

Lubrication reduces friction by putting a layer of oil or grease between the two moving surfaces as cartoon **C** shows. A thin film of oil often less than one hundredth of a millimetre thick is enough to reduce heat and wear in (for example) car engines running at 10 000 revolutions per minute!

**C**    *Lubrication*

**Viscosity** is a measure of how easily an oil will flow. (See cartoon **D**.) A 'thick' oil has a high viscosity. A 'thin' (runny) oil has a low viscosity. As oils are heated they become 'thinner'; their viscosity is lowered.

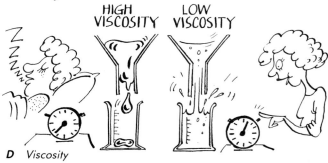

**D**    *Viscosity*

The Society of Automotive Engineers test viscosity and give the oil a number, e.g. SAE 40.
Low viscosity oils e.g. SAE 10, SAE 20 are used in light machinery. Medium viscosity oils e.g. SAE 30, SAE 40 are used in engines etc. High viscosity oils e.g. SAE 60, SAE 70 are used in gearboxes etc. Multigrade oils e.g. SAE 20–50 have a low viscosity when cold and a high viscosity when hot.

## Bearings

Bearings are used to support moving surfaces with reduced friction and wear.

Plain bearings or brushes (see diagram **E**) may be made of nylon, aluminium or brass and are basically a piece of material with a hole drilled in it. They are useful at low speeds and loads and inexpensive.

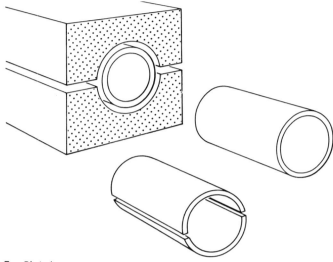

*E    Plain bearings or bushes*

Ball bearings or roller bearings (see diagram **F**) support a moving shaft on hardened steel balls or rollers held in a cage. They are more expensive but reduce friction better than plain bearings.

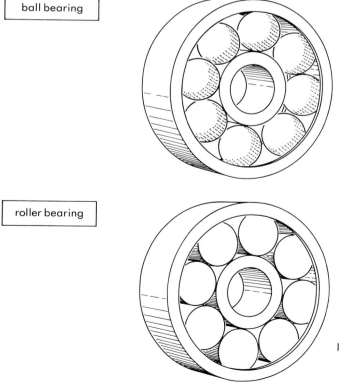

ball bearing

roller bearing

*F    Ball bearings or roller bearings*

## ▶ Things to do

▶ **1**   Copy cartoons **A** and **C**. Write three sentences about each.

▶ **2**   Rearrange the following mixed up sentences and write them out correctly.
   **a** Polished, move more, surfaces, easily
   **b** surfaces are more, Soft, to slide, difficult
   **c** force pushing the, reduces friction, Reducing the, surfaces together
   **d** the force, tends to stop, Friction is, which, surfaces, sliding
   **e** heat and, can lead, to, wear, Friction

▶ **3**   **Learn a skill – How to 'lubricate' (reduce friction in) the following materials:**
   **a** Wood (table top)      — wax
   **b** Sheet steel             — oil
   **c** Skin                       — soap
   **d** Bicycle wheel          — ????
   **e** Plastic curtain track  — ????
   Find out how to apply lubricants **a–c**. Suggest lubricants for **d** and **e**.

▶ **4**   **Think of a problem**   Design a device which uses each of the methods of lubrication shown in diagram **G**.

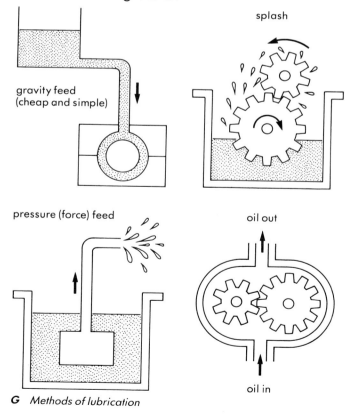

*G    Methods of lubrication*

▶ **5**   **Solve a problem**   Design (and carry out) an experiment to measure the viscosity of several liquids (water, parafin, machine oil, engine oil etc).

# 9.1 Electricity

**A** Forms of electricity

Electricity is a natural force. Lightning, and the static electricity when you brush your hair are both forms of electricity (see photographs **a**). Electrical energy comes from the movement of particles called **electrons**. A force called the **electromotive force** (e.m.f.) can be used to push electrons around a **circuit** made up of wires and electrical **components**. The e.m.f. is measured in **volts**. Electricity may be stored in **batteries** which usually have quite a low **voltage** (1.5 V, 9 V or 12 V). The electricity which is supplied to our homes is called **mains electricity** and has an e.m.f. of 240 volts. Diagram **B** shows how mains electricity is generated and distributed.

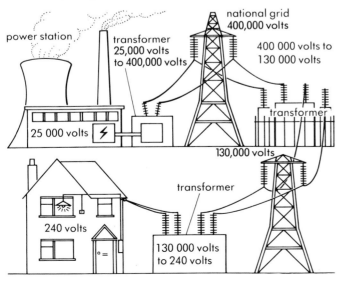

**B** Where mains electricity comes from

## Conductors and insulators

Materials which allow electrons to flow along them are called **conductors** of electricity. Copper is a very good conductor. Materials which prevent the flow of electrons are called **insulators**. PVC is a very good insulator. Electrical wires are usually made of copper with an insulating layer of PVC around them. Switches have conductors in the 'working bit' and insulation on the outside (see diagram **C**) so that you don't get an **electric shock**. Mains electricity of 240 volts is powerful enough to kill. So is a lower voltage at sufficiently high current.

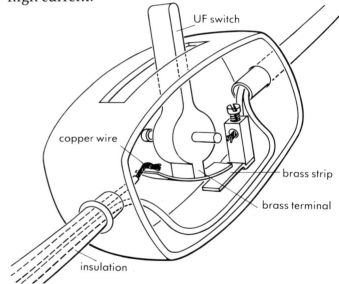

**C** A switch

Electricity flows from one terminal (the **negative** terminal) of a battery to the other (the **positive** terminal). The rate at which it flows is called **current** and is measured in **amperes** or **amps**. The battery e.m.f. can either push a small amount of electrons through a wire for a long time, or a large amount for a short time. A car battery (12 V) can keep a 5 amp parking light going for hours or a starter motor going just a few seconds on a cold morning when it demands 200 amps! Diagram **D** may help you understand the idea.

The amount of electricity which flows depends on the e.m.f. and the **resistance** of the components in the circuit to the flow. This is written as a formula

**e.m.f. (volts) = current (amps) × resistance (ohms)**

$$V = I \times R$$

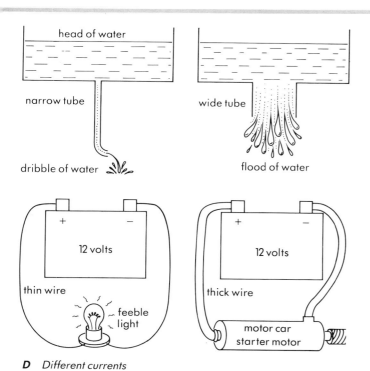

D   Different currents

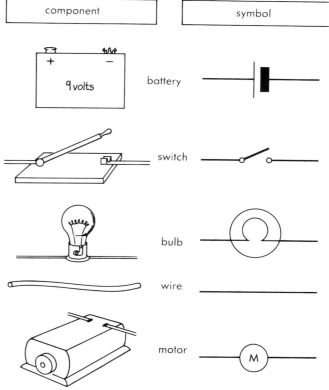

| component | symbol |
|---|---|

battery

switch

bulb

wire

motor

F   Circuit symbols

Drawing circuits as in Diagram **E** is slow and **circuit diagrams** are normally drawn using symbols for the components. Diagram **F** shows some of the more common symbols used. Components may be joined one after the other in a **series** circuit or side by side in a **parallel** circuit. Diagram **G** shows two simple circuits.

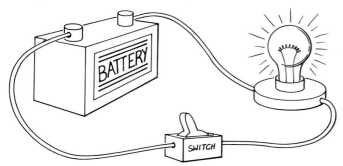

E   A circuit

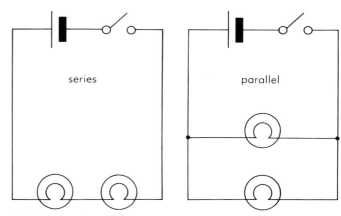

series

parallel

G   Series and parallel

## *Things to do*

1   Copy diagrams **F** and **G**.

2   Write two sentences about each of the following:
   **a** e.m.f.
   **b** conductors
   **c** insulators
   **d** circuits
   **e** mains electricity

3   **Learn a skill – How to calculate resistance**
   **a** Write the formula $V = IR$
   **b** This can be rearranged to calculate resistance: $R = V/I$

   **c** If a 12 volt battery causes a current of 3 amps to flow, what is the resistance of the circuit in ohms?

▶ 4   **Think of a problem**   Find a problem in the classroom which could be solved by an electrical circuit. Design the circuit.

▶ 5   **Solve a problem**   Draw a circuit diagram of a battery, two switches, two bulbs and a motor so that when one switch is turned on, one bulb will light and when the other is turned on, the other bulb will light and the motor will run.

# 9.2  Electronics

Electricity is about the movement of **electrons** and the study of electricity is called **electronics**. By using various electronic devices, the flow of electricity can be controlled in all sorts of ways. Diagram and photograph **A** shows some electronic components.

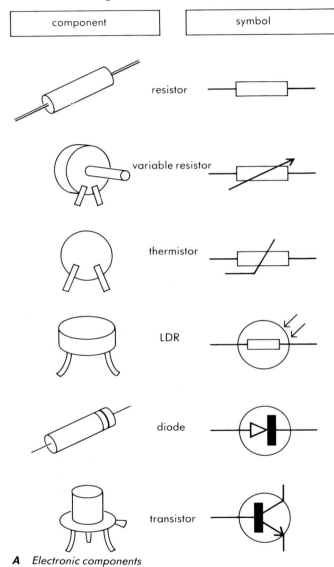

| component | symbol |
|-----------|--------|

*A   Electronic components*

**Resistor** – controls the flow of current
**Variable resistor** – variable control of current
**Thermistor** – resistor which changes resistance depending on temperature
**LDR** (light dependant resistor) – resistor which changes resistance depending on the light level
**Diode** – only allows current to flow one way through it
**Transistor** – an electronic switch and amplifier

A resistor can be used to reduce the current flowing to a bulb making it less bright (see diagram **B**). A variable resistor gives you more control over the current. In circuit **C** you can make the light bright or dim.

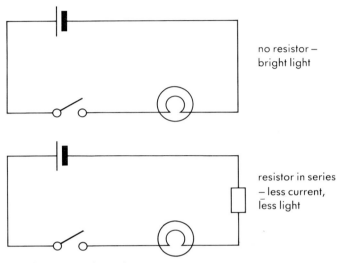

no resistor – bright light

resistor in series – less current, less light

*B   A resistor reduces the current*

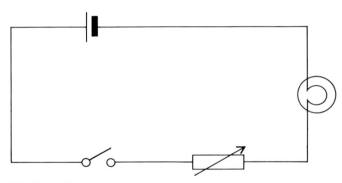

*C   A variable resistor controls the current*

If you put an LDR in the circuit the bulb's brightness will vary according to the light around it (**ambient** light) (see diagram **D**). One slight problem is that the bulb's light becomes brighter as the surroundings become brighter.

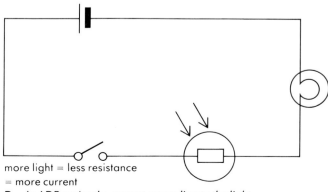

more light = less resistance = more current

*D   An LDR varies the current according to the light*

This would not be suitable if you wanted an automatic control for house lights! As we do not know much about electronics we can use the 'black box' principle and just draw a box, call it something like 'inverter' and pass our basic design (see diagram **E**) on to an electronics expert!

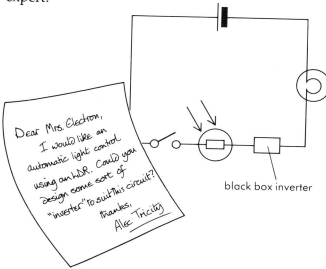

Dear Mrs. Electron,
I would like an automatic light control using an LDR. Could you design some sort of "inverter" to suit this circuit?
thanks,
Alec Tricity

black box inverter

*E*   *Call in the expert!*

## Transistors

A transistor has three wires coming out of it – **emitter, collector, base** (see diagram **F**). The base current controls the resistance of the transistor. The current flowing through the collector and emitter is switched on and off by the base current. A very small current flowing through the base to the emitter 'switches on' the main current through the collector/emitter. This produces a more sensitive circuit.

By using combinations of electronic components, circuits can be made up to control lights, open garage doors when you blow the horn, take in the washing when it rains and so on. Diagram **G** shows an electronic circuit for automatically drawing the curtains when it gets dark.

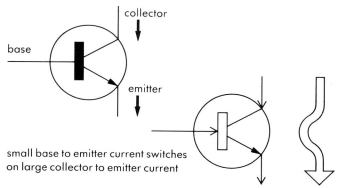

*F*   *How a transistor works*

## ▶ *Things to do*

▶ **1**   Match the heads to the tails and write out the sentences correctly.

| Heads | Tails |
|---|---|
| **a** A resistor | resistor allows you to control current. |
| **b** A variable | an electronic switch or amplifier. |
| **c** An LDR | allow current to flow one way. |
| **d** A transistor is | (light dependent resistor) is affected by light. |
| **e** A diode will only | controls the flow of electric current. |

▶ **2**   **a** Draw the following components and their symbols:
  **i** resistor,
  **ii** variable resistor,
  **iii** LDR,
  **iv** transistor,
  **v** diode.
  **b** Draw a simple circuit diagram for each to explain its effect.

▶ **3**   **Learn a skill – How to 'read' an electronic circuit diagram**
  Draw the circuit in diagram **G**. Study it carefully and label each component. Try to work out how it works. Write a simple explanation.

▶ **4**   **Think of a problem**   Find an application for an electronic circuit including a **thermistor**. When the ambient temperature is low the thermistor's resistance is high. Write about it and design the circuit (use black boxes for those parts of the circuit you cannot work out for yourself).

▶ **5**   **Solve a problem**   Your teacher wants a demonstration circuit to demonstrate the use of each of the components in diagram **A**, separately and in various combinations. Design the circuit.

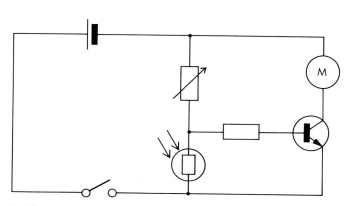

*G*   *The motor draws the curtains when it gets dark*

# 9.3 Microelectronics

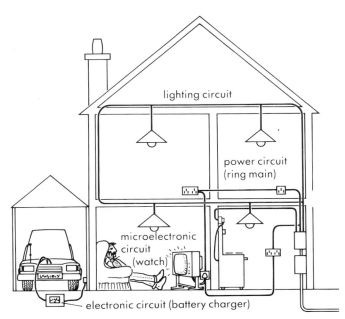

**A** Ring main circuits and microelectronic circuits

**Micro** means very small. Microscope, microorganism, micrometer all start with micro. Microelectronics uses electronic circuits which are very, very, small! Electrical circuits like a domestic ring main use large switches and bulb holders, thick wires and take up a lot of space. Electronic circuits are much smaller and use transistors, light emitting diodes (LEDs) and very thin wires or printed circuit boards (PCBs). Microelectronic circuits incorporate thousands of components and circuits in a single **microchip**. Diagram **A** gives some idea of the comparison of scale. Photograph **B** shows some of the components used.

The design of microelectronic circuits is a very specialist task. The process tends to go like this:

*Technologist*: I don't know anything about microcircuits, but I've heard that just about anything is possible.
*Microelectronics specialist*: Yup!
*T*: Well, I'm not happy with my mechanical watch. Is it possible to build an electronic watch?
*MS*: Yup! You just need a timing circuit, a transistor, capacitor and a few odds and ends.
*T*: Don't confuse me with details! So I need a timing circuit?
*MS*: Yup!
*T*: Now, could it also give me the date?
*MS*: Easy! and day and time in various time zones.

**B** Microchips

*T*: Where do you get all the components?
*MS*: Well, a chip which is made for computers can do all that and more. We just need to use part of its circuitry.
*T*: A computer chip! Hmm, does that mean you could make the watch a calculator as well?
*MS*: Yes, but we need a keyboard.
*T*: That's my problem. You get the chip, I'll get the keyboard. Let's start with black box problems (see diagram **C**).

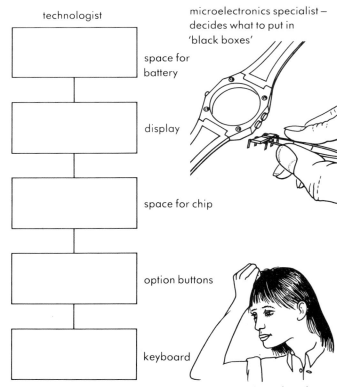

**C** What needs to go in the black box for a digital watch and calculator

Photographs **D** shows how a microchip is made.

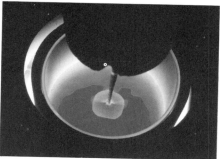

*D(i)*   The circuits are designed for the silicon chip

*D(ii)*   A small crystal of silicon is rotated in molten silicon, eventually forming a large cylindrical crystal

*D(iii)*   The crystal is sliced into wafers and the circuit transferred to the wafers

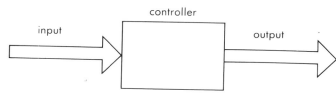

*D(iv)*   The wafers are coated in a furnace

*D(v)*   Industrial chips are cut from the wafers and mounted in plastic

Problems for microelectronics experts tend to be posed in terms of 'This is the **input**, I want that **output**'. For example 'I want a microelectronic device which will take the input of me flashing my headlights to give the output of the garage door opening ready for me to drive in'. In between input and output is a **controller** or **processing unit** as in diagram **E**.

controller

input → → output

*E*   The processing unit

To control room temperature you need a **sensor** to check on the temperature. The sensor needs to send an input signal to a unit which decides whether the temperature is too high or too low. If too high, then the output will be to turn the heating off. If too low, then the output will be to turn the heating on.

When designing a microelectronics circuit technologists tend to use **timer** circuits, **sensor** circuits, **control** circuits and build them up to solve the black box problems.

Inside a microchip there is a complicated pattern of pathways and components to control the flow of pulses of electricity. Microchips are made of silicon. Silicon is an element that is found in sand and clay. It can be treated to make different parts

of its surface have different electrical properties. If arsenic is added it makes what is called *n*-type material; if boron is added, *p*-type. These two types of material affect the flow in different ways. They are used to make transistors which act as switches or amplifiers of electrical signals. The transistors control speed, direction, size and effect of very rapid bursts of electricity. But before they can be used in a chip someone has to design the circuits.

## ▶ *Things to do*

▶ 1   Copy diagram **A** to show the differences in size between electrical, electronic and microelectronic circuits.

▶ 2   Draw a cartoon strip using photographs **D** as a guide to show how a microchip is made.

▶ 3   **Learn a skill – How to talk to a microelectronics technologist**
Write a 'script' for a conversation between a washing machine technologist and microelectronics technologist to arrive at a black box problem for a new automatic washing machine.

▶ 4   **Think of a problem**   Microcircuits are widely used now. Find a new use for a microcircuit.

▶ 5   **Solve a problem**   Design a new watch case to hold the battery, microcircuit, keyboard etc discussed in the text.

# 9.4 Computers

Diagrams **A–E** show ways in which calculators and computers can be used.

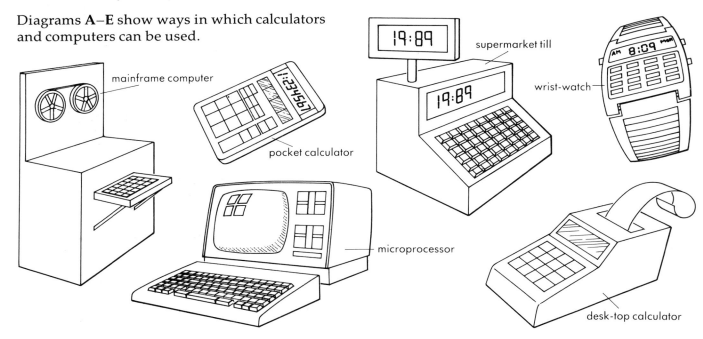

*A  Data processing machines*

## Computers

Computers are machines that work with ideas. Large ideas are made up of small bits called **facts**. Another word for facts is **data**. Computers use data to solve problems. Computers are very versatile machines and are used in technology as calculators, graphics aids, simulators, controllers and robots.

## Calculators

Modern technology is so complex that detailed calculations are essential. Powerful computers are invaluable for longer or quicker calculations.

## Graphics aids

Drawing by computer is fast, allows for easy changes of scale, rotation of drawings, changes of viewpoints etc.

## Simulators

Modern pilots are trained using computer simulations. The ability of the computer is to calculate what is happening very quickly and to 'draw' with computer graphics the result on a VDU screen. Computer games are simplified versions of these simulations.

## Computer control

Space travel involves very rapid responses to changing conditions. A landing on the moon or a rendezvous in orbit are so complex that it is doubtful whether these high technology developments would have been possible without computers. The control circuits in microwave ovens, washing machines and video recorders rely on microprocessors.

## Robots

Robots can work in unhealthy atmospheres and are accurate, reliable and untiring. Many production line jobs can be done by computers.

## Information processing

Handling orders, timetabling and the paperwork involved in modern shops, offices and industry is made easier by computers. Word processors are quicker and more versatile than typewriters and office work has changed very much with the introduction of computer technology.

As computers have been introduced, some firms have been able to reduce the number of people they employ. Many jobs have changed and some new jobs (in computer technology) have been created.

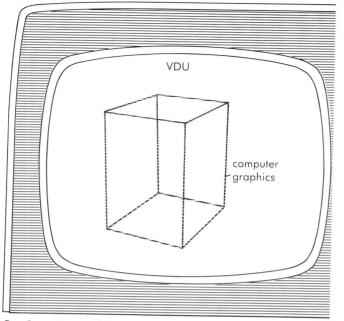

*B*  Computer graphics display

*E*  Booking tickets

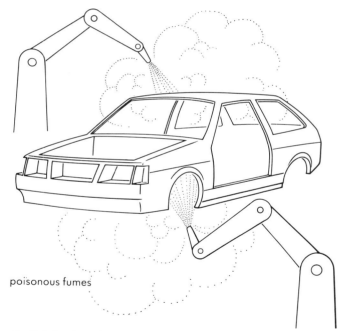

*C*  Painting by robots

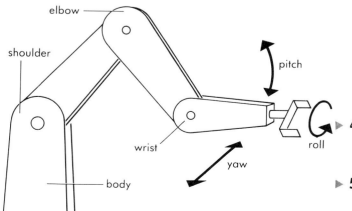

*D*  A robot arm

## ▶ *Things to do*

▶ **1**  Copy diagrams **A**, **C** and **E**.

▶ **2**  Write two or three sentences about the use of computers in:
  **a** calculation,
  **b** drawing,
  **c** simulation,
  **d** control,
  **e** robots.

▶ **3**  **Learn a skill – How to 'program' a robot**
All computers have to be programmed. Robots are computerised machines. Robots have various 'degrees of movement' – see diagram **D**. They also have to be programmed. Write a simple program to control a robot arm. You could start:
  **a** BEND SHOULDER
  **b** STRAIGHTEN ELBOW
  **c** BEND WRIST
  **d** ....

▶ **4**  **Think of a problem**  Think of a modern job which has not yet been computerised. Detail how a computer would help.

▶ **5**  **Solve a problem**  Write a short essay on the jobs lost through the introduction of computers, jobs gained and how computers can be used to help match workers with jobs.

# 10.1 Technology for museums

*A New and old machines*

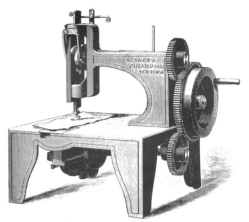

*A(i)   Isaac Singer's first sewing machine*

*A(ii)   A modern sewing machine*

*A(iii)   A washing machine, about 1895*

*A(iv)   The present-day washing machine*

People enjoy seeing old machines. Working models in museums and old factories are very popular. Photographs **A** show some old machines and their modern equivalents.

It is interesting and 'educational' to see how things were done in the past. Some people make money out of turning old industries into tourist attractions, see cartoon **B**.

Sometimes all that is left of old technology is a place name, ruined building or bump in the ground. People who dig to find out about the past are called **archaeologists**. Finding out about past technology is sometimes called **industrial archaeology**. Cartoon **C** shows some of the things that are useful if you want to find out about old local industries. **Maps** show sites of old factories, railway lines, mines and so on. Street names like Hot Water Lane may show a place where miners used to stop to wash on their way home in the past! **Telephone books** show all sorts of

industries. Old books show how businesses have changed and which ones have gone out of business. **Libraries** may have local history books and photos. **Your eyes and ears!** Look around you. Talk to people. Old folk are sometimes happy to reminisce about where they worked.

## Preserving the past

If you find an old machine do not just take it apart and throw it away! Take it to an expert who may be able to **restore** it. If you visit an old industrial site do not take home a souvenir unless you pay for it!

If there is an old factory or railway near you explore it carefully when you have permission. Make drawings, take photographs, report any interesting finds to your local museum but do not do any damage – the past cannot be replaced!

B New attractions

C How to investigate old industries

## ▶ Things to do

▶ **1** Choose one of the machines in photograph **A** and draw the old and the new versions.

▶ **2** Use cartoon **B** as a guide and draw a cartoon of your own to show how an old industry could be turned into a tourist attraction.

▶ **3** **Learn a skill – How to devise a set of safety rules**
Make a list of **ten** rules for visitors to the site of an old factory.

▶ **4** **Think of a problem**   Use diagram **C** for information and describe how you would find out about a disused railway line near you. Explain where you would go, who you would ask, what you would read and what you would do to record your findings. What problems would you expect to encounter?

▶ **5** **Solve a problem**   Imagine that you are responsible for setting up a local museum display of technology. Design a suitable display area, advertising poster and make sketches of the types of machines and models that you would use to make your display attractive and interesting. Diagram **D** may give you some ideas.

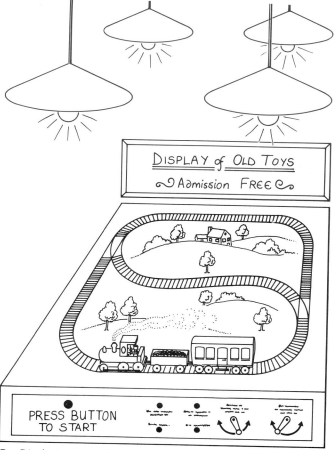

D Displaying technology

# 10.2 Appropriate technology

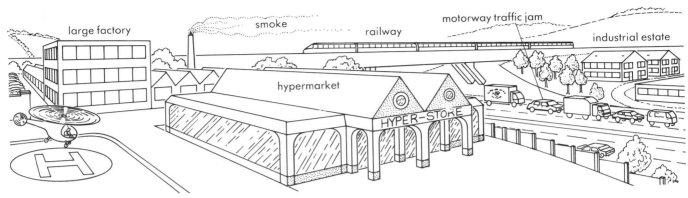

**A**  *Transport links*

Industrial nations such as Britain, USA, and Germany are **high technology** societies. They use cars, televisions, computers, microwave cookers, and so on. Industries in these countries use expensive, energy consuming, complicated and sophisticated machinery and processes. Transport systems include motorways, railways and aircraft which link cities of millions of inhabitants who work in these industries and consume their products (see diagram **A**).

The 'third world' of developing countries in Africa, India, South America and parts of Asia amount to three quarters of the world and tend to be **low technology** societies. Large parts of these countries have poor transport systems and standards of hygiene and the people are often illiterate. Eighty per cent of the people work on farms using primitive farming methods (see photograph **B**).

**B**  *Planting by hand*

People in the past have tried to help these countries by giving them tractors and farm machinery. These have failed because the local inhabitants cannot drive, petrol is scarce and expensive, roads are inadequate, mechanised farming causes unemployment and when they break down there are no skilled mechanics to repair them.

In 1963, Dr E. Schumacher invented the term **intermediate** technology to describe the process of using modern knowledge and experience to develop a technology to suit the people, resources and needs of a society. Intermediate technology fits between high technology and low technology. Most people now use the term **appropriate** technology to describe making technology appropriate to the country in which it is used.

Diagram **C** shows three different levels of farming technology. Diagram **D** shows appropriate improvements for each.

People interested in appropriate technology for developing countries now consider the needs of the country and the people, water and energy supplies, transportation, storage and marketing.

Before tackling any problem yourself, you must find out about the country, the people and the problems to be solved and the materials available locally.

Here are some typical problems which have been tackled: A hand-powered vehicle for disabled children in Southern India. A machine for counting tablets in a rural dispensary in West Africa. A simple lathe and forge made from oil drums. Simple scales for weighing babies.

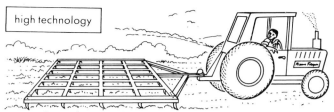

high technology

appropriate to large scale farming
quick but expensive to buy and maintain, may cause pollution

manual digging

low technology

broadcasting seed

labour intensive, hard work —
appropriate in some societies

intermediate technology

ox ploughing

low cost – appropriate in some developing countries

**C** Levels of technology

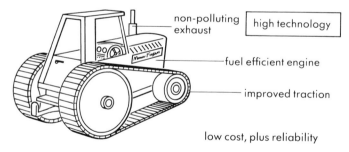

non-polluting exhaust

high technology

fuel efficient engine

improved traction

low cost, plus reliability

low technology

horse-drawn seed spreader

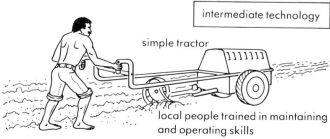

intermediate technology

simple tractor

local people trained in maintaining and operating skills

**D** Appropriate improvements

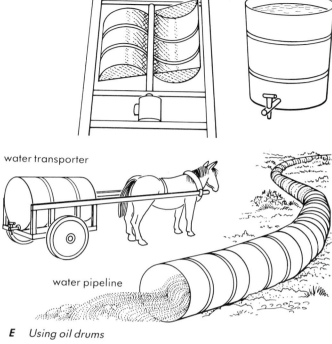

windmill

water butt

water transporter

water pipeline

**E** Using oil drums

## ▶ Things to do

▶ **1** Copy diagrams **C** and **D**.

▶ **2** Explain these words:
   **a** low technology,
   **b** high technology,
   **c** intermediate technology,
   **d** appropriate technology.

▶ **3 Learn a skill – How to write a specification for an appropriate technology problem**
Write a specification for a press to remove oil from groundnuts. You must mention who will use it, what sources of power are available, what the oil will be used for, how it is to be stored, how many nuts it must cope with, where it will be used, what materials are available, who will buy it, how it will be cleaned and so on.

▶ **4 Think of a problem** The introduction of machines to developing countries has led to the supply of oil drums. Empty oil drums are a new material available for use in solving problems. Diagram **E** shows some uses to which they have been put. Find another use for oil drums!

▶ **5 Solve a problem** Design a personal 'lorry'. It must be 3 m long, cost less than £500, have a fuel consumption of 80 km per gallon with no exhaust fumes. It should be able to be used on mud roads and in poor farming areas.

# 10.3  Pollution

**A**  *Pollution by technology*

All industrial processes produce waste products. In the past, technologists have been criticised (justifiably) for ignoring the effects of their actions on the environment. Open cast mining, smoke and smog, polluted rivers, and complete forests cut down are all examples of how the environment has been affected. Photograph **A** shows some of the polluting effects of early technologies.

A mixture of legislation and common sense has improved things since the 1950s. The murky, filthy, dense fog called **smog** which London used to suffer no longer occurs (Los Angeles still suffers!). Industries are quieter, less ugly and cleaner. Rivers are cleaner and oil spills are less frequent.

Pollution affects the **ecology** of the planet. If rivers are polluted, fish may be killed and they are certainly likely to move to cleaner water. A dead tree is eaten by wood lice and beetles which then become food for mice and voles which are later eaten by larger animals whose excrement keep the forest fertile in a natural **cycle**. A wooden lollipop stick also rots and **degrades**, but an empty plastic pop bottle will not usually rot – it is not **biodegradable**. Technology interrupts natural cycles.

Industries pump out carbon dioxide gas when they burn fuel and the $36 \times 10^{10}$ tonnes which have been formed in the last century have been partly absorbed by the oceans, but about half has remained in the atmosphere. The extra carbon dioxide may allow more radiated heat from the sun to reach the earth but forms an insulating layer preventing extra heat leaving. This is called

the **greenhouse effect** and has made the earth a warmer place, but what may be the effect in the future? Some technologists are very concerned about the **long term** effects on the planet (see diagram **B**).

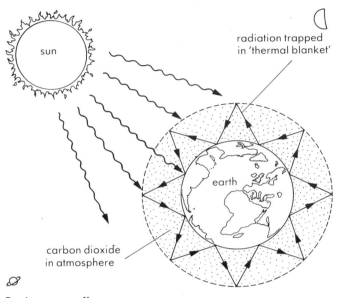

**B**  *Long term effects*

Technologies have now been developed to prevent pollution. Politicians have to decide whether they are used. Unleaded petrol causes less pollution and should perhaps be made compulsory; wind and water power is less polluting than coal and nuclear power but leads to visual pollution. The issues involved are complex.

Resources such as coal, oil, minerals and ores are being exploited at an increasing rate. Eventually we need to consider **conservation** of resources. Waste bottles can be saved in bottle banks, aluminium foil can be recycled and so on. The nuclear accident at Chernobyl (diagram **C**) and the longer term problem of **acid rain** (diagram **D**) affect people in countries neighbouring the source of the pollution. Countries now need to be good neighbours and to look at the **global implications** of their actions.

There are times when high technology has an **incidental**, unplanned and unexpected bonus. For example, motorways were thought to spoil countryside and have an adverse effect on plant and animal life. However, some wildlife can live happily around motorways.

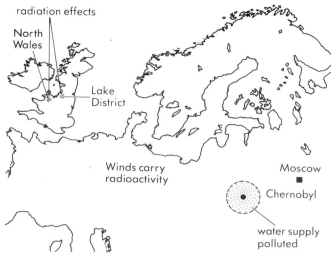

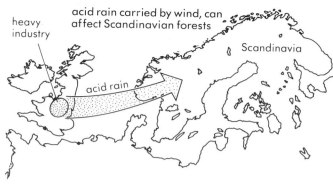

sulphur dioxide + water = sulphuric acid

*C    Effects of the Chernobyl disaster on the UK*

*D    Acid rain in Scandinavia from the UK's industry*

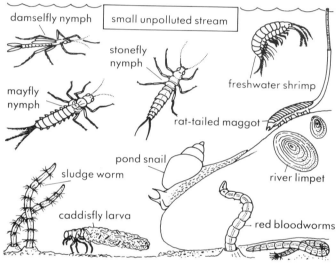

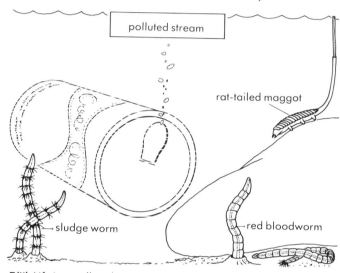

*E(i)   Stream life*

*E(ii)  Life in a polluted stream*

## Things to do

▶ **1**  Match heads to tails (**b** is done for you!)

| HEADS | TAILS |
|---|---|
| **a** Pollution problems can | wood does not pollute like non-biodegradable plastic. |
| **b** Ecology depends on | natural life cycles. |
| **c** Biodegradable | conserve resources. |
| **d** The greenhouse | be solved with existing technology. |
| **e** Recycling helps | effect is due to the $CO_2$ in the atmosphere. |

▶ **2**  Copy diagrams **C** and **D**. Write a paragraph about each to explain what has happened.

▶ **3**  **Learn a skill – How to detect pollution in rivers by studying the river life**
Diagram **E** shows the sort of creatures which normally live in a small British stream and the ones which can survive in a polluted stream. By studying the types of creature found, you can tell how polluted a stream is likely to be. If a study found a mayfly nymph, sludge worms, rat-tailed maggots and bloodworm in a stream would you think it was polluted, or not?

▶ **4**  **Solve a problem**   Carry out a school survey. Decide on two or three priority areas where pollution is a problem. Discuss the situation with friends, parents and teachers. Decide on measures to improve the environment of the school. Implement them and evaluate their success.

# 10.4 Jobs in technology

**A** Direct and indirect labour

Technology provides **goods** such as cars, computers and can openers. It also provides **services** such as education, entertainment and effluent disposal. Primitive people tend to have simple needs and low technology. They spend all their time providing goods and services for themselves **directly**. They farm, feed and forage. In more complex societies people specialise: they provide goods and services indirectly. Teachers teach the children of farmers who supply produce which is packaged by someone else, distributed and sold to others (see diagram **A**). This is called **division of labour**. Production of goods occurs in three areas:

**1 Primary production** – extraction of materials, farming and timber production (photographs **B**).
**2 Secondary production** – takes primary products such as iron, timber and meat and changes them to products for sale – cars, tables and tins of spam (photographs **C**).
**3 Tertiary production** – advertises products, delivers, arranges finance, entertains and educates (photographs **D**).

**B** Primary production

**C** Secondary production

**D** Tertiary production and services

In Britain, about half a million people are employed in primary production, three quarters of a million in secondary production and 15 million in tertiary production. Technology has helped change the **pattern of employment** (see diagram **E**).

Industry not only produces goods, but also thinks up new products in **research and development** departments. These products are sold by **marketing and sales** departments, creating money. This money is handled by **finance** departments to buy raw materials, pay bills, invest in the future and pay employees who are employed by **personnel** departments. Other departments look after stock, distribution, cleaning and secretarial work.

The 'family tree' below shows the range of departments in an industrial company.

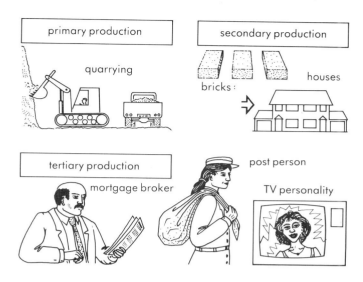

**E**   *The pattern of employment*

**Directors**

| Production | Research | Marketing | Finance | Personnel | Services |
|---|---|---|---|---|---|
| planning production inspection | research development design | marketing sales distribution | buying wages contracts | employment training welfare | secretarial cleaning transport |

**CURRICULUM VITAE**

Name

Date of birth

Education    from          to

Qualifications

Employment history

Hobbies and interests

Referees

**F**   *CV form*

## ▶ Things to do

▶ **1**  Copy the 'family tree' of a company.

▶ **2**  Write three or four sentences about each of the following:
   **a**  division of labour,
   **b**  primary production,
   **c**  secondary production,
   **d**  tertiary production,
   **e**  departments of a company.

▶ **3**  **Learn a skill – How to apply for a technological job**
   Use the curriculum vitae (CV) form (diagram **F**) to write your own CV and a letter of application for a job in technology.

▶ **4**  **Think of a problem**   Write an advertisement for a job in technology which you would want to apply for.

▶ **5**  **Solve a problem**   Where would you get information about technological jobs and further training opportunities?

# Technological achievements

**A** Telecom Tower, London

**B** Pont-Gysyllte Aqueduct, Wales

**C** The Parthenon, Athens

**D** Abraham Darby's iron bridge, Shropshire

**E** The Church of the Holy Sepulchre, Cambridge

**F** Stonehenge

**G** The Eiffel Tower, Paris

*H The Severn Bridge*

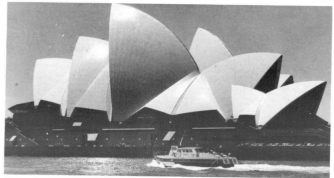

*I The Sydney Opera House, Australia*

*J The Pyramids of Giza, Egypt*

*K Crystal Palace, London*

*L Bodiam Castle, Sussex*

*M Steam train*

## ▶ *Things to do*

▶ 1 Put these technological achievements into 'chronological' order, starting with the oldest.

▶ 2 Choose five photos, and for each one explain the main technological problem to be overcome, e.g. when the Severn Bridge was built, the main problem was to design a roadway which could withstand the high winds in the channel and the heavy traffic flow between England and Wales.

▶ 3 Of the technological achievement shown here, which one do you think has been (or will be) the most useful? Give reasons for your choice.

# Safety

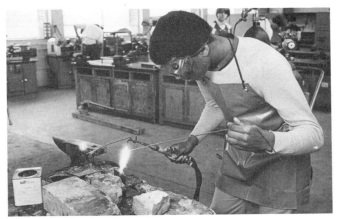

*A   School workshop*

*B   School science lab*

Safety is vital in technology as in all practical subjects. Photographs **A**, **B** and **C** show safe work places. Look after the workshop or laboratory. Clear up accidental spillages. Report hazards to the teacher and report breakages.

**Be sensible** – silliness causes most accidents.

**Wear appropriate clothing** – fashion clothes may not protect you should an accident happen. Be especially careful with jewellery, cuffs, ties, long hair etc. See cartoon **D** for the two extremes and photograph **E** for a real hero!

**Look after your tools and equipment** – always use the correct tools for the job. Worn or blunt tools are dangerous. Frayed cables can cause electric shocks.

*C   Building site*

**Take precautions** when you are working with particular machines or processes. Goggles should be worn when a using a lathe, a leather apron when welding and safety glasses when using acid.

Follow these safety rules:

| DO | DO NOT |
|---|---|
| Be careful | Act the fool |
| Be sensible | Rush your work |
| Wear an apron | Use any tools unless you have been shown how |
| Wear sensible shoes, remove any jewellery, tie back long hair | Touch power tools without permission |
| Report **any** accidents to the teacher | Talk to anyone who is using a machine |
| Wash your hands at the end of the lesson | |

> **REMEMBER**
> Carelessness causes most accidents
> The workshop is not dangerous – **you are**

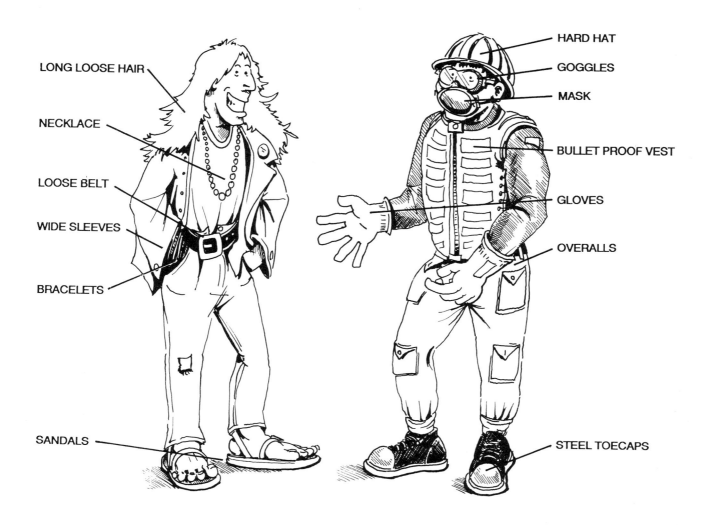

LONG LOOSE HAIR

NECKLACE

LOOSE BELT

WIDE SLEEVES

BRACELETS

SANDALS

HARD HAT

GOGGLES

MASK

BULLET PROOF VEST

GLOVES

OVERALLS

STEEL TOECAPS

**D**   *Two extremes!*

**E**   *Safety on the road*

# Class design activity – active learning/role play

**A** *Class discussion*

The idea of the activity is to involve the whole group in a design activity with the opportunity to extend into role play if this is thought appropriate.

## Sequence

1 **Teacher** leads class discussion (see cartoon **A**). Ten ideas for a **topic** for the **design competition** are put on the blackboard.

2 **Class** elects the following personnel:
   a 1 **Managing director** (the best organiser)
   b 1 **Secretary** (the neatest writer/drawer)
   c 3 **Design consultants** (best at design)
   d 3 **Tellers** (best at maths)

3 **Managing director** organises class vote on which topic to choose. **Secretary** helps by drawing up a choice table (see table **B**).

| Topic | Do-ability | Interest | Marketability |
|-------|-----------|----------|---------------|
| 1     |           |          |               |
| 2     |           |          |               |
| 3     |           |          |               |
| 4     |           |          |               |
| 5     |           |          |               |

**B** *Choice table*

**C** *Badges*

4 **Class** copies choice table and fills it in, giving each box a number, 0–5 in value
   $$0 = \textbf{poor} \quad 5 = \textbf{excellent}$$

5 **Tellers** collect the sheets and find best score.

6 **Class** 'does' chosen topic in groups. This follows the technological design process.

### DESIGN SHEET

**PRIZE CERTIFICATE**

Awarded on
this ..................................... day
of ..................................... 19 ........
to .....................................................
.....................................................
for the most wonderful design
for a ...............................................

**Design team:**

Freda Florence Fritz          Sir Fred Smith School

**D** *Design sheet*

7   **Managing director** designs **three** certificates for first, second and third prize groups. **Secretary** draws the certificates neatly ready for presentation. **Tellers** design judging sheets for elected **design consultants** to use when judging.

**E** *Prizegiving*

8   **Design consultants** judge designs, **tellers** tot up scores and **managing director** presents '**The grand prize certificates**'.

The success of this type of activity depends on planning and encouragement. The ideas in the diagrams may help sustain the sense of fun.

# Steps in technology – design game

## Aim

To simulate the stages a designer goes through to produce a successful design for **anything**.

## Instructions

Choose any number on a random number circle to start with. The next player takes the 7th number clockwise. **Good luck!!**

## Find a problem

Thinking time. Throw *4* or over to start.

## Search for information

**10*** See idea in a shop. Go forward *5* – or throw again (for a new design).

**14*** Use library. Go forward *4*.

**18*** Ask a craftsman. Go forward *6*.

## Wait to write specification

Any turn which lands on or above **30** must wait until the next throw to see how their specification is judged.

## Next throw

**Judgement by a Grand Old Designer.**

*1, 2* and *3*. Unsellable and impractical. Go back to **A.**

*4* or *5*. Too expensive. Stay at **C** for one more throw.

*6* or *7*. OK Go forward by your score.

*8* or *9*. **Great**. Go forward *10*.

## Start here

Use a scrap of paper as a counter.

| | | | | | |
|---|---|---|---|---|---|
| 1 *A* | | | | | |
| 2 | 3 | 4 *B* | 5 | 6 | 7 |
| | | | | | 8 |
| 14 * | 13 | 12 | 11 | 10 * | 9 |
| 15 | | | | | |
| 16 | 17 | 18 * | 19 | 20 | 21 |
| | | | | | 22 |
| 28 | 27 | 26 | 25 | 24 | 23 |
| 29 | | | | | |
| 30 *C* | 31 | 32 | 33 | 34 | 35 |
| | | | | | 36 |
| 42 | 41 | 40 | 39 | 38 | 37 |
| 43 | | | | | |
| 44 | 45 | 46 | 47 | 48 | 49 |
| | | | | | 50 |

## Wait to plan work

Any turn which lands on or beyond **58** must wait at **58** until they throw *5* or more. Then go forward that number.

## Wait here to start production

If you land on **70** or beyond, wait to throw *6* or more, then go forward by that number.

## Snag!

Plastic factory burns down. Return to **70**.

## Evaluation

If you land on **98** or beyond – WAIT! This is the crunch! Does it sell? Your next throw will tell you.

*1* or *2*. Not strong enough. Keeps breaking down. No sales. Go back to **18**.

*3* or *4*. Lots of complaints. Go back to **30**.

*5* or *6* or *7*. Minor complaints. Go back to **58** and improve your design.

*8*. Great – but you have copied someone else's design. Legal action started against you. Sorry! Go back to square **2**!

*9*. *JACKPOT* – Sells like hot cakes. No complaints. Retire on fortune to design Great New British Successes. Go to **100**!

| 56 | 55 | 54 | 53 | 52 | 51 |
|----|----|----|----|----|----|
| 57 | | | | | |
| 58  | 59 | 60 | 61 | 62 | 63 |
| | | | | | 64 |
| 70  | 69 | 68 | 67 | 66 | 65 |
| 71 | | | | | |
| 72 | 73 | 74 | 75 | 76 | 77 |
| | | | | | 78 |
| 84 | 83 | 82 | 81 | 80 | 79 |
| 85 | | | | | |
| 86  | 87 | 88 | 89 | 90 | 91 |
| | | | | | 92 |
| 98 *G* | 97 | 96 | 95 | 94 | 93 |
| 99 | | | | | |
| 100 | Jackpot! | | | | |

# Glossary

**Alloy** metal made of two or more elements e.g. steel (iron and carbon), solder (lead and tin) (4.1)
**Anneal** heating and then cooling slowly to soften a metal (4.1)

**Belt drive** plastic or rubber belt being used to drive a shaft (7.3)
**Bevel gear** gear with teeth set at an angle (7.3)
**Blast furnace** a furnace where a blast of air is used to increase the temperature (3.4)
**Brief** short summary of a technical problem (2.1)
**Bush** plain bearing usually made from nylon or brass (8.4)

**Cam** shaped shaft used to make a component move in a particular way (7.4)
**Chain drive** a chain running on a sprocket used to transmit drive (7.3)
**Compression** pressing together (8.1)
**Conductor** material which allows electricity or heat to flow through it (e.g. copper) (8.1)
**Connecting rod** rod which connects two components e.g. piston and crankshaft (7.4)

**Development** trying out and improving ideas and solutions to problems (2.3)
**Ductility** ability to be stretched without breaking (8.1)

**Ecology** the study of how plants, people and animals affect each other and the environment (10.3)
**Efficiency** how well something works (6.3)
**Electron** negatively charged particle (9.1)
**Energy** ability to do work (5.1)
**Engine** device which can do work (7.1)
**Engineer** someone who can design and make (2.2)
**Evaluate** assess how well or badly something has been made or works (2.4)

**Ferrous metal** a metal containing iron (e.g. steel) (4.1)
**Flow chart** diagram of movement of people or things in a process (2.1)
**Friction** force between moving surfaces which tends to slow them down (8.4)
**Fuse** an electrical safety device (9.1)

**Galvanise** coat with zinc to prevent rusting (8.3)
**Gear** toothed wheel used to transmit motion (7.3)

**Gear train** several gears moving in mesh with one another (7.3)

**Heat treatment** heating and cooling a metal to change its properties (4.1)
**Horsepower** unit of measurement of power (6.2)

**Industrial revolution** time when Britain became industrial rather than rural (7.1)
**Industry** trade and manufacture, often using machines (2.2)
**Insulator** material which does not allow electricity or heat to flow through it (e.g. PVC) (8.1)

**Knot** defect in timber where a branch has been cut (3.1)

**Lever** bar which rests on a pivot and is used to move a load (7.2)
**Linear** in a straight line (7.4)

**Machine** device for applying power (7.1)
**Mains** the electricity supply to a house (240 volts) (9.1)
**Malleability** ability to be hammered into thin sheets without cracking (8.1)
**Metallurgy** the science of metals (4.1)
**Model** representation of a proposed design or system (2.2)

**Neutron** electrically uncharged particle (9.1)

**Ore** minerals containing metal or metal compound (3.4)

**Pollution** contamination of the environment (10.3)
**Power** ability to exert a force (7.1)
**Production** making something for use (2.4)
**Proton** positively charged particle in nucleus of atom (5.3)
**Prototype** a trial model or first version (2.2)
**Pulley** grooved wheel for cord to pass over to change direction of a force (7.3)

**Ratchet** mechanism to allow movement in one direction only (e.g. on a fishing spool) (7.4)
**Reinforced concrete** concrete strengthened with steel rods to improve tensile strength (4.4)
**Rotary** circular motion (7.4)

**Scale model** a model that is larger or smaller than the final product (2.4)
**Science** study of a branch of knowledge (1.1)
**Scientist** someone who can do experiments to extend knowledge (1.1)
**Smelting** process of extracting metal from ore by heating (3.4)
**Solder** alloy of lead and tin used in plumbing (4.1)
**Specification** detailed description of the construction of an item (2.1)

**Technical** applied scientific skills (1.1)
**Technician** someone who is expert in practical techniques (1.1)
**Technology** practical applications of science (1.1)
**Technologist** someone who uses scientific knowledge to solve practical problems (1.2)

**Tempering** a reheat process following hardening to remove internal stresses (4.1)
**Tension** pulling apart (8.1)
**Thermoplastic** plastic which can be softened by heat and reshaped (3.3)
**Thermosetting** plastic which cannot be reshaped by heating (3.3)
**Torque** turning force (7.2)

**Weld** join together by heating until materials melt (8.2)
**Work** work is done when a force moves an object (5.1)
**Working model** a model that moves (2.4)
**Workmanship** a person's skill in producing a well finished article (2.4)

# Useful data

## Properties of some common metals

| Material | Chemical symbol | Density (how 'heavy' is 1 cm³ of the metal?) g/cm³ | Coefficient of linear expansivity × $10^{-6}$/°C (how much longer does it grow when heated by 1 °C?) | Melting point °C |
|---|---|---|---|---|
| Aluminium | Al | 2.7 | 23 | 660 |
| Copper | Cu | 8.9 | 17 | 1083 |
| Gold | Au | 19.3 | 14 | 1000 |
| Iron | Fe | 7.9 | 12 | 1535 |
| Lead | Pb | 11.3 | 29 | 327 |
| Mercury | Hg | 13.6 | 60 | −38 |
| Nickel | Ni | 8.9 | 13 | 1458 |
| Zinc | Zn | 7.1 | 30 | 419 |

## Metals in the earth (by weight)

| | |
|---|---|
| Aluminium | 8% |
| Iron | 5% |
| Magnesium | 2% |
| Chromium | 0.02% |
| Nickel | 0.008% |
| Tin | 0.004% |
| Lead | 0.002% |
| Uranium | 0.0004% |
| Silver | 0.00001% |

## Properties of some common non-metal materials

| | Density | Coefficient of linear expansivity × $10^{-6}$/°C |
|---|---|---|
| Softwood | 0.5 | 3.0 |
| Glass | 2.2 | 8.5 |
| Acrylic | 1.2 | 0.8 |
| Polystyrene | 1.1 | 0.7 |

## Twist bits for pilot and shank holes for screws

| Shank number | 2 | 4 | 6 | 8 | 10 | 12 |
|---|---|---|---|---|---|---|
| Shank hole diameter mm | 2.3 | 3.2 | 4.0 | 4.8 | 5.6 | 6.4 |
| Pilot hole diameter mm | 0.8 | 1.0 | 1.5 | 2.0 | 2.5 | 3.0 |

## Choosing adhesives

|  | Wood | Metal | Glass | Ceramic | Fabric | Paper | Plastic | Stone |
|---|---|---|---|---|---|---|---|---|
| Wood | 1 | 2,3 | 2,3 | 2 |  |  |  |  |
| Metal | 2,3 | 2,3 | 3 | 2,3 |  |  |  | 2,3 |
| Glass | 2,3 | 3 | 3 | 2,3 |  |  |  | 2,3 |
| Ceramic | 4 | 1,2 | 2 | 1,2 |  |  |  | 3 |
| Fabric | 1,2,5 | 2 | 2 | 2 | 5 | 1,5 | 2 | 4 |
| Paper | 1,2,6 | 2 | 2 | 1,2 | 2,5 | 1,2,6 | 2 | 1,2 |
| Plastic | 2,3 | 2,3 | 2,3 | 2,3 |  |  | 2,3 | 4 |
| Stone |  | 3 | 3 | 2,3 |  |  |  | 2,3 |
|  |  |  |  |  |  |  |  | 3 |

| Adhesive | Strength | Water resistance | Setting time (hours) | Brand name |
|---|---|---|---|---|
| 1 PVA | Very good | Poor | 1 | Evo Stick Woodwork |
| 2 Contact | Very good | Good | 0.25 | Impact/Bostik 1,3 |
| 3 Epoxy resin | Excellent | Excellent | 1–12 | Araldite, Bostik 7 |
| 4 Mastic | Good | Good | Varies | Bostik flooring adhesive |
| 5 Latex | Good | Good | 0.25–1 | Copydex |
| 6 Paste | Good | Poor | 0.5 | Lion, Polycell |

## Resistor colour code

| Colour | First band | Second band | Third band |
|---|---|---|---|
| Black | 0 | 0 | |
| Brown | 1 | 1 | 0 |
| Red | 2 | 2 | 00 |
| Orange | 3 | 3 | 000 |
| Yellow | 4 | 4 | 0000 |
| Green | 5 | 5 | 00000 |
| Blue | 6 | 6 | 000000 |
| Violet | 7 | 7 | |
| Grey | 8 | 8 | |
| White | 9 | 9 | |

e.g. red, red, red = 2 200 $\Omega$ = 2.2 k$\Omega$
red, black, yellow = 200 000 $\Omega$ = 200 k$\Omega$

## Binary numbers

| Decimal | Binary |
|---|---|
| 0 | 00000 |
| 1 | 00001 |
| 2 | 00010 |
| 3 | 00011 |
| 4 | 00100 |
| 5 | 00101 |
| 6 | 00110 |
| 7 | 00111 |
| 8 | 01000 |
| 9 | 01001 |
| 10 | 01010 |
| 11 | 01011 |
| 12 | 01100 |
| 13 | 01101 |
| 14 | 01110 |
| 15 | 01111 |
| 16 | 10000 |